HARMONY
WITH GOD

HARMONY WITH GOD

A Fresh Look at Repentance

By

ZANE C. HODGES

REDENCIÓN VIVA
· P.O. Box 141167 · Dallas · Texas · 75214 ·

Cover by Martin Massinger

Scripture taken from The New King James Version.
Copyright © 1982 by Thomas Nelson, Inc.
Used by permission. All rights reserved.

Copyright © 2001, by Kerugma, Inc. All rights reserved.

No part of this publication may be reproduced, stored in a retrieval system, or transmitted in any form or by any means—electronic, mechanical, photocopy, recording, or any other—without prior permission in writing from Kerugma, Inc., except in the case of brief quotations.

ISBN 1-879534-04-5

CONTENTS

1. Repentance Reconsidered:
   Repent *and* Believe? 1
2. Arguments from Silence—
   and All of That 5
3. To Repent or Not to Repent:
   John's Doctrine of Repentance 13
4. The Ninety-Nine Righteous
   Sheep: Repentance in Luke 15:1-10 23
5. Lost Son, Not Lost Sonship:
   Repentance in Luke 15:11-24 31
6. The Self-Righteous Older
   Brother: Repentance in Luke 15:25-32 39
7. Unless You Repent:
   Repentance in Luke 13:1-5 49
8. Repentance and the Day
   of the Lord: 2 Peter 3:9 57
9. New Birth, Forgiveness
   and Repentance 65
10. Harmony with God 77
11. Repentance in Palestine 89
12. Repentance and Sound Doctrine 109

Scripture Index 125

This book is dedicated to my friend

Steven G. Rowe, Sr.

and my many friends at

Coast Bible Church

—1—
REPENTANCE RECONSIDERED: REPENT *AND* BELIEVE?

If someone were to ask you, "What must I do to be saved?" what would you say? Many preachers and lay Christians today would probably say, "Repent of your sins and believe on the Lord Jesus Christ." Of course there are plenty of people who would give other, more complicated answers than this one. But we are not concerned with those other answers in this booklet.

We are, however, concerned with the statement, "Repent and believe." It is obvious that such a statement lays down *two* conditions for eternal salvation, namely, repentance and faith. The number of people who believe that *both these conditions* must be met is very large indeed.

But those who give this reply should do so with a twinge of conscience. Quite obviously they are not giving the answer which Paul and Silas gave to the Philippian jailer who asked that very question: "Sirs, what must I do to be saved?" (Acts 16:30). Their answer

Harmony with God

said absolutely nothing about repentance. Instead they gave the famous and simple reply, "Believe on the Lord Jesus Christ, and you will be saved" (Acts 16:31). Of course, people who believe the Bible do not want to be charged with contradicting the Bible. So most of those who insist on repentance as a necessary condition for salvation would claim that they are not *really* contradicting Paul and Silas. Many who deny any contradiction claim that repentance is somehow or other implicit in Acts 16:31. But it is truly difficult to see how such a claim can be demonstrated.

Equally to the point is another hard fact. The Gospel of John, which claims to be written to bring men to faith and eternal life (Jn 20:30-31), never once even mentions repentance. Still less does it make it a condition for eternal life along with faith. If John had really believed that to be saved one must "repent and believe," it staggers the mind to consider that he never manages to say so in 21 chapters of his Gospel. By contrast, he says over and over again that one must *believe*.

Once again, supporters of the "repent and believe" doctrine frequently say that repentance is "implicit" in John's Gospel. But this claim bears all the earmarks of what is called "eisegesis"—the process of reading into a text what one wants to find there, even when it is obviously not there. No interpreter of Scripture should be allowed this privilege unless he can show that in some way the text itself demands an implicit idea that is not directly expressed.

Of course, all texts, whether human or divinely inspired, work on assumptions that are not always directly stated. But this fact does not relieve the interpreter from

> "THE GOSPEL OF JOHN, WHICH CLAIMS TO BE WRITTEN TO BRING MEN TO FAITH AND ETERNAL LIFE, NEVER ONCE EVEN MENTIONS REPENTANCE."

demonstrating that these assumptions do indeed underlie the text he is considering. And it is nothing less than a monumental task to show, if repentance is truly a condition for eternal life, that the text of the Gospel of John clearly requires us to understand this. Nothing is less probable on its face than the claim that John omits any mention whatever of a fundamental condition for eternal salvation in a book in which he seeks to bring people to that salvation (John 20:30-31).

It is the claim of this book that no such demonstration is possible, either in Acts 16:31, in the Gospel of John or anywhere else in the New Testament. The bottom line is that repentance is *not* a condition for eternal life, and that faith alone is the sole condition on which human beings are eternally saved.

—2—
ARGUMENTS FROM SILENCE— AND ALL OF THAT

In *Absolutely Free! A Biblical Reply to Lordship Salvation* (Dallas: Redención Viva, 1989), I stated that the silence of the Gospel of John about repentance was "the death knell for lordship theology" (p. 148). That statement remains true today.

However, some individuals within the Free Grace Movement have raised the objection that this claim is an "argument from silence" and therefore invalid. This, however, is not the case. In the first place, we do not really have here an argument *from* silence, but an argument *about* silence. The issue is: W*hy* is John silent about repentance in the Fourth Gospel?

A classic "argument *from* silence" would run like this: "Our historical data for (let us say) the period 1168 BC to 1068 BC is sketchy and incomplete, so Arabia could have been a major regional power during that time." The argument is worthless, of course. The silence of our historical data tells us nothing about the power status of Arabia during the period described.

Harmony with God

The present issue is not comparable, as the following discussion will show.

In the second place, it is important to note that those who might reject the argument about the absence of repentance in John's Gospel are not claiming *not to know* John's view of repentance. On the contrary, they are making a *direct claim* about John's theology!

For example, lordship people claim that, *of course*, John held that repentance was necessary to salvation. They usually add that, though he does not mention it explicitly, repentance is there *implicitly*. But the search for "implicit" indicators of repentance in John's Gospel becomes a hopeless hodgepodge (forgive the expression) of guesses and misguided creativity.

On the other hand, many good people in the grace camp maintain that "repentance" can mean simply a "change of mind." Therefore, when a person turns from unbelief to faith in Christ, he or she has "repented" because they have changed their minds about Christ and about how people receive eternal salvation. The grace people who hold this "change of mind" view of repentance insist that John really *did* believe repentance to be necessary to eternal life, but simply chose never to state it explicitly. From this perspective, repentance automatically happens when one believes. John knew this, but never said so!

If *my* view of John's silence is an argument from

silence, so is this by all means!

So you can see my point when I say that the argument is really an argument *about* John's silence. *Why* was he silent on this major biblical theme?

An Illustration

Let me illustrate. Suppose a cardiologist wrote a book called *Significant Treatments for Heart Disease*. (I have recently acquired an interest in cardiology and the Lord has provided me with a good heart doctor.) Let us now suppose that in the course of his lengthy book, this cardiologist referred to angioplasm, cholesterol-reducing drugs, and Dr. Dean Ornish's plan for reversing heart disease without surgery or drugs. But suppose he referred not even once to heart bypass surgery. Would we not find this surprising?

The absence of any reference to heart bypass surgery in a book on *Significant Treatments for Heart Disease* would literally cry out for explanation. We could, perhaps, conclude that the author was poorly informed and incompetent. But if we knew otherwise, his silence about this widely used medical procedure would carry profound implications. The most obvious explanation for such a silence by a trained professional would be that he held that "heart bypass" surgery was *not significant*, no matter how widely used.

Harmony with God

Someone may reply that it is inconceivable that a trained writer could write such a book in the present medical climate. The widespread use of this surgery would virtually compel some reference to it by the author, whether he approved of it or disapproved. Not to mention it would not be a reasonable option. (In fact, Ornish's book *does* mention heart bypass surgery and elaborates on its drawbacks. See Dr. Dean Ornish's *Program for Reversing Heart Disease* [New York: Ivy Books, c. 1990, 1996].)

This only strengthens my case.

Those who claim that repentance is necessary for salvation (even in the sense of a "change of mind") have every reason to be uneasy and perplexed about John's silence. Especially so in the light of our Lord's command in Luke 24:47 that "repentance and remission of sins *should be preached* in His name to all nations, beginning at Jerusalem" (italics added).

John certainly does not *preach* repentance in his Gospel! You don't *preach* a truth by being silent about it. One needs only to compare this with how explicit Peter is on this subject in Acts 2:38 and 3:19 (not to mention Paul on Mars Hill, Acts 17:30).

The verb used in Luke 24:47 and translated "preach" is the Greek verb *kerusso*, meaning "to proclaim aloud, announce, mention publicly, preach." If anyone knows how to "preach" a truth without ever mentioning it by

Arguments From Silence

name, please write to me in care of Redención Viva!

A False Premise

The whole problem we are discussing is due to a false premise. The false premise is this: *repentance is necessary for eternal life.*

No medical professional today would dream of writing a book on *Significant Treatments for Heart Disease* without mentioning bypass surgery precisely because in the context of modern medicine this is a significant treatment in the view of most medical professionals. Only if most medical professionals agreed that bypass surgery was not significant, would it make sense to write a book ignoring it.

In the same way, if no New Testament apostle or prophet held that repentance was necessary for eternal life, then John would have no reason to mention it when telling people how to obtain that life. This explanation—and this only—fits the facts naturally.

This is why I refer to the view that "repentance is necessary for eternal life" as a false premise. This view is in reality a *petitio principii*—that is, a begging of the question. It cannot be demonstrated from Scripture.

Let's put it this way. If we *started* with the Gospel of John, would we have any reason from the Gospel itself to suppose that repentance was necessary for

Harmony with God

eternal life? The obvious answer is no.

Why then do we think that John included it implicitly in his Gospel? Because we bring to the Gospel the untested and unprovable assumption that *other* New Testament texts show that repentance *is* necessary. Apart from this false premise, John's silence about repentance is both easily explained and extremely natural.

During the course of this booklet, we will look at virtually every text that might be claimed as proof that

> **"NO TEXT IN THE NEW TESTAMENT (NOT EVEN ACTS 11:18) MAKES *ANY DIRECT CONNECTION* BETWEEN REPENTANCE AND *ETERNAL* LIFE. NO TEXT DOES THAT. NOT SO MUCH AS ONE!"**

repentance is necessary for eternal life. I have also covered much of that ground in chapter 12 of *Absolutely Free!* But let us simply state here what we will be affirming in the following discussions:

No text in the New Testament (not even Acts 11:18) makes *any direct connection* between repentance and *eternal* life. No text does that. Not so much as one!

Arguments From Silence

Conclusion

We ought, therefore, to reexamine our ingrained assumptions about New Testament repentance. I know how hard this is for preachers, teachers and lay people who have long believed and/or taught otherwise. I myself once held the "change of mind" view of repentance and taught it.

But the Scriptures have persuaded me otherwise. So I invite the reader of this booklet to consider the Scriptures with me and to be open to the teaching of the Holy Spirit.

—3—
TO REPENT OR NOT TO REPENT: JOHN'S DOCTRINE OF REPENTANCE

In the last chapter, we considered the fact that John is silent in his Gospel on the subject of repentance. In view of the purpose of the Gospel of John to bring people to eternal life (Jn 20:30-31), we were constrained to conclude that John did not regard repentance as a condition for eternal salvation.

John is also silent about repentance in his three epistles. This is an interesting fact to which we will return later in this chapter.

But John is far from totally silent on the subject of repentance. In fact, he refers to it no less than a dozen times in the book of Revelation. It is surprising to realize that John has more references to the subject of repentance than any New Testament writer except Luke!

The author who ranks third in references to repentance is Matthew (8 times). But all other writers

Harmony with God

trail Luke, John, and Matthew by a considerable distance.

Mark has only 4; Paul in all of his thirteen letters only 5; the author of Hebrews 3; and Peter 1. Jude has none.

These counts are based on the actual number of occurrences of the Greek noun (*metanoia*) and verb (*metanoeo*) for repentance. Even if we also count *metamellomai* (a less common word for repentance), Matthew only gains 3 uses, Paul 1 and the writer of Hebrews 1. Paul also has 2 uses of *ametameletos* (= "not to be repented of").

John's showing here is impressive, considering that all of his references are confined to one book. It seems clear that if we examine the dozen uses in Revelation, we ought to get a fairly definite idea about John's own doctrine of repentance.

Repentance for the Saved in Revelation

It is striking that eight of John's twelve references to repentance (all using the Greek verb *metanoeo*) are found in the letters to the seven churches. There is no good reason to take any of these references to unsaved people, and plenty of reason to refer them to the saved.

For example, in Rev 3:14-22 our Lord rebukes the church of Laodicea for being spiritually "lukewarm."

To Repent or Not to Repent

Then in v 19 He states: "As many as I love, I rebuke and chasten. Therefore be zealous and repent." The reference to chastening here recalls the teaching of Heb 12:3-11 and clearly shows that the Laodiceans are the Savior's beloved children whom He desires to correct. They can avoid His chastening if they *repent!*

To the same effect is Rev 3:3. The Lord has just declared to the Christians of Sardis that "I have not found your works perfect [Greek = complete] before God" (3:2). He then commands them to "remember therefore how you have received and heard; hold fast and repent." On its face it is plain that these are Christians who have actually labored for the Lord but whose works for Him are not yet complete. They have been overtaken by a spiritual deadness, or lethargy (cf. 3:1), from which they need to arouse themselves. They need to "be watchful, and strengthen the things which remain" (3:2) and "hold [them] fast" (Greek = "guard" or "keep" [them]). But to do this they need to *repent* of the deadness of their present experience (cf. James 2!), which was threatening the loss of their previous accomplishments for God (cf. 2 Jn 8).

That this is an experience appropriately applied to true Christians alone, is a fact that will probably only be denied by teachers of lordship salvation! Very obviously, John is not telling these people that what they *really* need to do is to *believe and be saved.* If anyone

Harmony with God

can find *that* in this text, he is a magician!

Basically the same thing can be said of the remaining references to repentance in the letters to the seven churches. The Christians in Ephesus have "left" their "first love" (Rev 2:4). Their original devotion to Christ has died down. So the Lord says to them: "Remember therefore from where you have fallen; repent and do the first works, or else I will come to you quickly and remove your lampstand from its place—unless you repent" (2:5). The future of the Ephesian church as a witness for her Lord depended on whether the Christians there would *repent* of their cooling devotion to the Son of God and resume their previous vigorous activity for Him.

In the church at Pergamos (Rev 2:12-17) there were those who held false doctrine that encouraged compromise with pagan immorality and idolatry (2:14-15). The church is called upon to repent of its toleration for such teaching, and warned that otherwise the Lord will deal with these people Himself (2:16).

Finally, the female teacher in the church at Thyatira, who called herself a prophetess (Rev 2:20), had been warned to repent of the immoral conduct to which her false teaching led, but she had failed to repent (2:21). For this reason, the woman herself would be disciplined by sickness (2:22; cf. 1 Cor 11:30), and her followers in the church would experience great tribulation, or trouble, "unless they repent[ed] of their deeds" (2:22). No one here was threatened with hell, but simply with severe discipline.

The early church did indeed have female prophets, as is made plain by Acts 21:9 and 1 Cor 11:5. Whether the woman designated as "Jezebel" in Rev 2:20 was a true prophetess by spiritual gift and now claimed to utter prophecies that God had not given to her, or whether she was not a gifted prophetess at all, it is not possible to say. But that she was also unsaved goes far beyond anything indicated in the text. Even the false teachers, Hymenaeus and Alexander, are treated by Paul as subject to discipline to purge them from blasphemy (1 Tim 1:20; cf. *The Gospel Under Siege*, 2nd ed. [Dallas: Redención Viva, 1992], pp. 83-84).

The New Testament plainly recognizes that some false teachers (though not all) are Christians who have gone far astray and will perhaps only be recovered by severe discipline. There is nothing to show that the "Jezebel" of Thyatira (probably not her real name) was not one of these. The statement of her impending punishment strongly suggests that John thought of her as a Christian who had seriously strayed from God. Despite God's longsuffering patience, she had ignored her opportunity to *repent* and now faced His approaching discipline.

In these eight occurrences of the verb "to repent"

in the letters to the churches, not so much as one of them suggests the idea of turning from unbelief to faith in God or Christ. In every case a particular failing of some duration is the object of the repentance that our Lord commands.

The words *of some duration* are deliberately chosen. In every case in Revelation 2 and 3 something has gone wrong with either the attitude or the behavior (or both) of some (or all) of the Christians in these churches. Significantly there is no call to repentance in the letters to the churches at Smyrna (2:8-11) and Philadelphia (3:7-13). The reason is obvious: there is nothing about which these churches need to repent!

This is obviously the reason for the absence of a call to repentance in 1 John. The church, or churches, addressed (perhaps the leaders are chiefly in view) are in excellent spiritual condition (cf. 1 Jn 2:12-14, 21) and need simply to "remain" (= "abide") in the truth and in fellowship with their Lord (2:24, 28). The same may be said of the church addressed in 2 John and of Gaius, who is addressed in 3 John.

As John's use of repentance in Revelation 2 and 3 makes clear, repentance is for those Christians who have in some way gone astray. The issue is not some failing which is immediately addressed by confession (1 Jn 1:9). The issue is always some prolonged attitude or practice. The same view of repentance is found in

To Repent or Not to Repent

Luke 15 which we will address in subsequent chapters.

Repentance for the Unsaved in Revelation

There are four uses in Revelation of the Greek verb for repentance (*metanoeō*) which are clearly applied to the unsaved. These are: Revelation 9:20-21 and 16:9, 11. What is remarkable about these uses is that *they too* refer to repentance from long-held sinful attitudes or practices. In no case is there a reference to repentance from *unbelief*.

In Revelation 9:20-21 the list of things not repented of is long: "But the rest of mankind . . . did not repent of the works of their hands, that they should not worship demons, and idols of gold, silver, brass, stone, and wood . . . And they did not repent of their murders or their sorceries or their sexual immorality or their thefts." This is pure and simple an assertion that the unsaved did not repent of *their sins*. And this unrepentance was maintained in the face of the devastating plagues of Revelation 8 and 9, and in particular the plague of Rev 9:13-19, by which a third of the world's population is killed (Rev 9:18)!

In Revelation 16:9, as men are scorched with heat from the fourth bowl judgment, "they blasphemed the name of God who has power over these plagues; and they did not repent and *give Him glory*" (italics added)!

Harmony with God

Put another way, they refused to stop blaspheming and withheld the glory which was due to Almighty God (cf. Rom 1:21). In Revelation 16:11, under the fifth bowl judgment, men "blasphemed the God of heaven because of their pains and their sores, and did not *repent of their deeds*" (italics added).

> "IN REVELATION REPENTANCE IS *ALWAYS* RELATED TO GOD'S TEMPORAL JUDGMENTS, WHETHER OF HIS OWN PEOPLE OR THE WORLD AT LARGE."

Clearly there is nothing in these texts about repenting of *unbelief!* In fact, mankind actually *believes* that God is behind these plagues and they refuse to change either their attitude or their ways. For this reason, God's judgments continue to fall. There is no issue in these texts that pertains directly to eternal salvation. The issue is plainly unrepentant behavior which justifies the *temporal judgments* of God.

In Revelation, therefore, repentance is *always* related to God's temporal judgments, whether of His own people or the world at large. This is John's clear doctrine of repentance. Repentance is never related by John to obtaining eternal life.

To Repent or Not to Repent

Conclusion

Many very fine grace people have held the view that the apostle John, at least in his Gospel, regarded repentance as a "change of mind" that turned one from unbelief to faith in Christ. However, it is impossible to find such a doctrine of repentance anywhere in John's writings.

The view that repentance is sometimes a virtual synonym for saving faith is without any evidence in John's five New Testament books. In future chapters I hope to show that this concept of repentance cannot be found anywhere in the New Testament. Instead, the doctrine of repentance as found in Revelation is in fact the teaching of all the New Testament authors.

—4—
THE NINETY-NINE RIGHTEOUS SHEEP: REPENTANCE IN LUKE 15:1-10

Just as 1 Corinthians 13 is the classic New Testament chapter on love, and Hebrews 11 is the classic chapter on the life of faith, just so Luke 15 is the classic chapter on repentance. The three parables that it contains are familiar and much loved. They are, of course, the Parable of the Lost Sheep, the Parable of the Lost Coin, and the Parable of the Lost Son.

It is a great irony, however, that these three stories are very often misread and misunderstood. This irony is even greater in view of the fact that the text of Luke gives us a clear and unmistakable clue to their meaning. In this chapter we shall consider the first two of these stories as they are found in Luke 15:1-10. In the following chapter, we will look at the Parable of the Lost Son, while in the one after that we will consider this son's self-righteous older brother.

Harmony with God

The Parable of the Lost Sheep

The three parables of Luke 15 are introduced by verses 1-3. There we see the Pharisees and scribes complaining that our Lord Jesus "receives sinners and eats with them" (v 2). They are scandalized by the fact that He accepts them into table fellowship with Himself. This no self-respecting Pharisee would condescend to do. In response to their criticism, Jesus proceeds to tell these stories, beginning with the Parable of the Lost Sheep.

It is clear on the face of this story that the shepherd of this parable owns all one hundred sheep. This is plain in the words, "What man of you, having a hundred sheep" (v 4) and from the words "my sheep" in verse 6. As was frequent in Palestine, especially in the southern region called the Negeb (= "the dry"), this shepherd was grazing his flock in territory described as "the wilderness." This sparsely inhabited region contained sufficient vegetation to sustain sheep as their shepherd led them from grazing place to grazing place. Thus, in the parable, the shepherd is feeding his sheep when he notices that one of them has wandered away from his flock.

Upon making this discovery, he leaves the ninety-nine "in the wilderness" in order to "go after the one which is lost" (v 4). From the perspective of a Middle

The Ninety-Nine Righteous Sheep

Eastern shepherd, this can hardly mean anything other than that he felt the flock was reasonably safe and would stay together.

After recovering the lost sheep, he places it lovingly "on his shoulders" (v 5) and brings it back to the flock. When the day's grazing is over and "he comes home" (v 6), he has a party to which he invites "his friends and neighbors" (v 6) so they can share his joy in having "found my sheep which was lost" (v 6). That this "party" parallels the celebrations staged in the next two parables, goes without saying.

Our Lord's application of this story is crystal clear: "I say to you that likewise there will be more joy in heaven over one sinner who repents than over ninety-nine *just* [Greek, *dikaios* = righteous] *persons who need no repentance*" (v 7; italics added). The words which we have placed in italics are the key to this parable. The ninety-nine sheep represent people who are "righteous" and who therefore do not need to repent. This is what the text plainly states.

But this is not how it is interpreted by many who read and/or teach it. Instead, the "ninety-nine just persons who need no repentance" are transformed into "ninety-nine unrighteous persons who only think they need no repentance!" That this manifestly contradicts the text and turns it upside down is so clear that this rereading of our Lord's words is self-refuting.

Harmony with God

Plainly stated, the Parable of the Lost Sheep is not about eternal salvation at all. It is about a Christian who wanders away from God's flock and pursues the pathway of sin. His restoration to fellowship with his Savior and Shepherd, as well as to fellowship with the Lord's people, who have not wandered away, requires repentance. When such a recovery of a straying believer occurs, the Great Shepherd is filled with joy and heaven itself rejoices with Him. And so, of course, should God's people as well (a point to be addressed in the story about the brother of the Prodigal Son: Luke 15:25-32).

After more than 40 years of ministering to the group of believers who now gather at Victor Street Bible Chapel, I am thankful that the Lord has allowed me to see this parable fulfilled repeatedly. Time after time, various ones of God's straying sheep have been found and restored to the flock by their loving Shepherd.

The Parable of the Lost Coin

Our Lord's second parable in Luke 15 reinforces as well as complements the first. If the Shepherd Himself is concerned for any of His sheep that stray, so also the Christian Church should be. As has often been suggested, the woman in this parable is very naturally taken as representing the Church itself.

The Ninety-Nine Righteous Sheep

Once again, it is obvious that the woman of the parable is the person to whom the ten coins belong. One of them becomes lost (v 8), but just as clearly the other nine do not! The story assumes that the woman knows exactly where they are. She is looking for the one lost coin, not the other nine.

In order to find it, however, she must "light a lamp" and use a broom to "sweep the house" (v 8). It is evident that the place where she lives is both dark and dirty, and that she believes the lost coin may be found in

> **"BORN-AGAIN CHRISTIANS DO INDEED GO ASTRAY IN THIS WORLD OF DARKNESS AND FILTH, BUT THEY STILL RETAIN THEIR IDENTITY AND VALUE TO GOD..."**

some dark nook or cranny where there might be considerable dirt or trash. The parable thus admirably fits the reality that the Christian Church lives in a world which contains more than enough spiritual darkness and moral filth (cf. 2 Pet 1:19 "as a light that shines in a dark place").

Born-again Christians do indeed go astray in this world of darkness and filth, but they still retain their identity and value to God just as a lost coin is still valuable no matter how much trash it is buried under.

Harmony with God

The Church is responsible to recognize, as did the woman in the parable, that the straying Christian still has enormous value and needs to be returned to the company of other believers so that his value and theirs may be properly utilized for God. A Christian church is always "richer" when a straying Christian returns to the fold.

The recovery of such a Christian is a source of joy to the Church and to its heavenly "friends and neighbors," the angels of God (vv 9-10). That the angels are intimately concerned with what happens in the Christian church is clearly indicated by passages like Ephesians 3:10; 1 Corinthians 11:10; Hebrews 1:14; 12:22-23; and other texts. Indeed, 1 Corinthians 11:10 in particular implies that the angels observe Christian practices and activities (cf. also Lk 24:6-7). Employing the imagery of the Lord's parable, we might say that whenever the Church gathers the angels are "invited" and in fact attend as unseen guests! So whenever the Church gathers and rejoices over a backslidden believer who has been recovered, it does so "in the presence of the angels" who are there to share that joy (v 10)!

Conclusion

There is nothing at all in either parable about eternal

The Ninety-Nine Righteous Sheep

salvation. In fact, Luke 15 as a whole is a celebration of one of the most joyous experiences that a Christian congregation can have—the recovery for God, and for the congregation, of one of God's precious sheep and valued coins. May the Lord grant this joy repeatedly in grace churches all over the world!

The misreading of the parables of Luke 15 as though they applied to the salvation of sinners is very unfortunate. To be sure, it is wonderfully joyful when an unsaved sinner gets saved. That joy too has come many, many times to Victor Street Bible Chapel. But it is not the joy described in these parables about repentance. To be saved, all the unsaved person needs to do is to believe on the Lord Jesus Christ (Acts 16:31)!

—5—

LOST SON, NOT LOST SONSHIP: REPENTANCE IN LUKE 15:11-24

Luke 15 is the classic NT chapter on repentance. Here, if anywhere, we should meet the fundamental teaching on NT repentance. As we saw in Luke 15:1-10, in the previous chapter, the first two parables of the chapter—The Lost Sheep and The Lost Coin—very clearly refer to the repentance of a born again person who has wandered away from God's flock and has become "lost" in the sense of being out of touch with the Lord and His people.

A Son Before He Repented

But if this is evident in the first two parables, it is even more evident in the third parable, The Prodigal Son. Indeed the very title by which this parable is known in the church declares the parable's clear intent. This is the story of a son who has wandered away from his

Harmony with God

father! The NT does not disclose any sense in which unregenerate people may be regarded as "sons of God." It follows, therefore, that the reference is to a Christian who has gone astray, just as the lost sheep and the lost coin have exactly the same reference.

It is notable that even in the far country where the Prodigal squanders his resources, he is fully conscious of his sonship. We are told: "But when he came to himself, he said, 'How many of *my father's* hired servants have bread enough and to spare, and I perish with hunger! I will arise and go to *my father*, and will say to him, "*Father*, I have sinned against heaven and before you, and I am no longer worthy to be called *your son*. Make me as one of your hired servants"'" (Lk 15:17-19; emphasis added). Are these the words of an unsaved person? Hardly.

Even after squandering the resources that his father had placed in his hands, the Prodigal is still fully aware that he is his father's son. He is also aware of the lofty privilege of being a son, but he now feels that his conduct makes him unworthy of such a status. He intends to tell his father to reduce him to the level of a hired servant, not because he is not a son, but because he feels "no longer worthy *to be called* your son." We hear an echo of these words in the lovely statement of 1 John 3:1: "Behold what manner of love the Father has bestowed upon us, that we *should be called* children

Lost Son, Not Lost Sonship

of God!" (italics added). The Prodigal feels he has fallen far below the privilege of being called a child or son of his father.

The repentant Prodigal now goes back home and is welcomed unconditionally by his father who "ran and fell on his neck and kissed him" (v 20). The son's confession is genuine but he underestimates the fullness of his father's forgiving grace. So he not only says, "Father, I have sinned against heaven and in your sight," but he also adds, "and am no longer worthy to be called your son" (v 21).

The father brushes such an idea aside, however, and he says, "Bring out the *best robe* and put it on him, and put a ring on his hand and sandals on his feet" (v 23, emphasis added). This is not the treatment accorded to hired servants! And the father also says, "And bring the fatted calf here and kill it, and let us eat and be merry; for *this my son* was dead and is alive again; he was lost and is found" (vv 23-24; italics added). Both in terms of his treatment of the Prodigal, as well as by his direct announcement, the father proclaims the returning young man to be his son.

But it should be noted carefully that he is not *just now* becoming his son. On the contrary this same son, previous to this moment, had been "dead" and "lost," but is now "alive" and "found." These words of course do not mean that this son had somehow literally lost his

Harmony with God

life. Instead they describe his period of separation from his father. On the level of the entirely human experience in this parable, the father has felt the absence of his son as deeply as if he had died, because he had totally lost contact with him. Their reunion is like a glorious coming to life and a joyful rediscovery of the shared father-son experience. Any father who has long been separated from a son whom he loves dearly can fully relate to these words.

An Enormous Waste

Once this parable is properly understood as applying to the restoration of a straying Christian, its vital lessons leap to life. To begin with, just as the Prodigal "wasted his possessions with prodigal living" (v 13), so also the straying Christian wastes the resources God has placed in

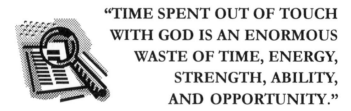

"TIME SPENT OUT OF TOUCH WITH GOD IS AN ENORMOUS WASTE OF TIME, ENERGY, STRENGTH, ABILITY, AND OPPORTUNITY."

his possession. Time spent out of touch with God is an enormous waste of time, energy, strength, ability, and opportunity. When such a Christian is restored to the Lord, he often experiences profound regret for what has been wasted during his period of separation from God. This is

Lost Son, Not Lost Sonship

especially true when the separation has lasted for years, as it sometimes does. I actually know fellow Christians who have expressed exactly this realization to me.

A Deep Sense of Unworthiness

In returning to God, particularly after a long separation from Him, repentant Christians are likely to experience a deep sense of unworthiness. They may feel that they have disgraced the Christian name and they may be all too aware of bringing disrepute to God their heavenly Father. Such Christians need to be reassured of the full and gracious acceptance God extends to them when they return. Their forgiveness is complete and they need not feel as if they are forever second-class Christians, as if they now served God as mere hired servants. Instead they should be encouraged to enjoy all the privileges of sonship, symbolized by the robe, the ring, and the sandals.

Lost Opportunities

But as is transparent from the story, though the Prodigal returns to the full experience of sonship, he does not get back the possessions he has foolishly squandered. Restoration for the straying Christian is real, but the loss of time, potential, and opportunity is equally real. The portion of any Christian's life that is spent away from

Harmony with God

God, as well as the rewards that might have been earned during that time, are permanently lost.

A Time to Rejoice

But though all this is true and sobering, it does not destroy the reality of the joy that should always be a part of the "home-coming" of a repentant son. The parable assures us that God our Father always rejoices when one of His sons comes home. And if He does, so should we.

No Grounds to Doubt

Finally, as this story shows, if the gospel is properly understood, the backsliding Christian will have no grounds to doubt his salvation, even when he is in the far country of sin. Like the Prodigal himself, he will still know that he is a son of the Father whose fellowship he has left. Needless to say, this assurance can be a powerful incentive for the backslider to "go home"!

Years ago, I heard a young man in a Baptist church up north give his testimony about returning to God from a deeply backslidden condition. But he assured us that he always knew he was a Christian because he had learned with regard to salvation that "there was

Lost Son, Not Lost Sonship

nothing I could do to earn it, and nothing I could do to lose it!" If all churches taught the gospel that clearly, they would lay a solid foundation for the return of more than a few prodigal sons!

—6—
THE SELF-RIGHTEOUS OLDER BROTHER: REPENTANCE IN LUKE 15:25-32

As we have seen in our last two chapters, Luke 15 is not at all about the repentance of unsaved people. On the contrary, the chapter is about the repentance and restoration of Christians who have wandered away from their Shepherd and His flock (15:4-7), from their place and role in the Christian church (15:8-10), and from fellowship with God their heavenly Father (15:11-24). The final section of Luke 15 furnishes us with a vital and instructive postscript, or addendum, to our Lord's teaching on Christian repentance.

As the older brother of the prodigal son returns from his work in the field, he hears the sounds of the celebration inside the house. Upon inquiring, he is told their significance: "Your brother has come, and because he has received him safe and sound, your father has killed the fatted calf" (15:27). The older son is far from pleased with this information about his father's party

Harmony with God

for his younger brother. In fact, "he was angry and would not go in" (15:28). As his subsequent words make plain, he is not really angry with his *brother*, but with his *father* for giving him such a lavish welcome.

In short, he does not share the joy that his father feels on this occasion.

The older brother thus represents a type of Christian whose attitude toward a wayward Christian brother is far less charitable than is that of God, his heavenly Father. The successors of the older brother in this parable have been numerous in the history of the church. Let us look at this brother's attitude more carefully.

The father of the angry brother is gracious enough to come out to talk to him, and his dad "pleaded with him" to join in the celebration (15:28). Although he might well have *ordered* his son into the party, that would have been foreign to the whole tenor of the occasion. God Himself, of course, has no intention of commanding us to feel joy for the restoration of a wayward Christian brother, since true joy must necessarily be spontaneous. Needless to say, such joy must always spring from the work of the Holy Spirit in our hearts.

We Shouldn't Overestimate Our Service

The Self-Righteous Older Brother

The complaint of the older brother is very instructive. He begins with an assertion of his own faithful service to his father by saying, "Lo, these many years I have been serving you; I never transgressed your commandment at any time" (15:29a). Clearly this brother is quite self-satisfied with the performance of his duties on the farm. No doubt he *had* worked for his father for a long time, but we may be permitted to doubt the full truth of his sweeping claim that he "never . . . at any time" had disobeyed his father. True, he had never left home as his brother had done, but to claim that he had never violated a commandment from his father was no doubt going too far.

Christians who have long served God run a serious risk of falling into the psychological and spiritual trap in which this older brother was caught. We may sweepingly survey our years of service as praiseworthy while conveniently forgetting the numerous failures, large and small, that have occurred over those years. It is even surprising how committed Christians can sometimes rise to high levels of indignation about the failures of others in the church when, in fact, perhaps years ago they themselves exhibited the same or similar failures. In their criticism of others, they may exhibit a lack of patience or compassion of the type they themselves once needed both from God and from their fellow believers.

Harmony with God

The danger of becoming self-righteous about our Christian commitment is quite real and our memories often conveniently block out recollections that might seriously puncture our self-satisfied perspective. Indeed, we can sometimes even forget our *present* deficiencies and failures!

We Shouldn't Criticize Our Father's Actions

This attitude is bad enough, but the older brother now goes further with what amounts to an accusation against his father. For now this self-righteous man declares: "[I did all this] and yet you never gave *me* a young goat, that I might make merry with *my* friends" (15:29b; italics added). Like almost all self-satisfied people, this brother feels that his father has given him less than he deserves. Not only has the fatted calf never been killed for him, he has never even been given a *young goat* for a party!

In the same way, self-righteous Christians often feel aggrieved that God has not blessed or rewarded them more lavishly than He has. In fact, if there is some hardship in the self-righteous person's life, he is likely to feel that he deserves "better than this" from the God whom [he thinks] he has served so well!

Such people entirely miss the spirit that our Lord Jesus Christ enjoined on His disciples when He said:

The Self-Righteous Older Brother

"So likewise you, when you have done all those things which you are commanded, say, 'We are unprofitable servants. We have done what was our duty to do'" (Lk 17:10). Obviously this is a far cry from the older brother's arrogant criticism of his father.

There is a kind of irony in the fact that the older brother does not express a desire to "make merry with" his *father*, but rather he wishes to do that with his *friends* (v 29). He is way out of touch with his father's heart on this occasion and he does not think in terms of sharing his parent's joy, but simply doing something with people of like mind with himself. This is a tragic outlook indeed!

Sadly, the self-righteous Christian is often very much at home in the company of other self-righteous people with whom he can spend time commiserating about the low estate of the church, the faults of other believers, etc. Were God Himself to walk in on such a gathering, it would "spoil the fun" since the spirit of the self-righteous critic is truly a great distance removed from the spirit of a loving heavenly Father who longs for the return of His wayward children.

We Should Heed Our Father's Gentle Rebuke

The father's rebuke of his angry older son is gentle but firm: "Son, you are always with me, and all that I have is yours" (v 31). "Have you forgotten your advantages?" the father is asking. "You enjoy my presence at all times, and you are also my heir." With these simple words, the father delineates the sharp contrast between his older and younger sons.

The younger son *had left* his father's presence for a long time, accumulating all the pain and suffering that

> "THERE IS NO REASON FOR BELIEVERS TO RESENT A STRAYING CHRISTIAN WHO RETURNS TO THE FOLD. SUCH CHRISTIANS HAVE SUSTAINED REAL AND TANGIBLE LOSSES THAT OBEDIENT CHRISTIANS DO NOT EXPERIENCE."

his prodigal lifestyle had wrought. Moreover, he had squandered his inheritance since the money he had asked for and used was "the portion of goods that falls to me" (see 15:12). The inheritance of the older son was still fully intact. There was no need for him to feel resentment and jealousy simply because his father was having a celebration for his repentant son. The disadvantages of those wasted years were very real for the Prodigal Son. The older brother was far ahead of the game simply because he had stayed home.

There is no reason for believers to resent a straying

The Self-Righteous Older Brother

Christian who returns to the fold. Such Christians have sustained real and tangible losses that obedient Christians do not experience. They have thrown away "treasures in heaven" which they could have been accumulating during their wayward years. Moreover they have lost the personal experience of the presence of God, for although He has always been with *them,* they have not been *with Him* in the sense of enjoying His fellowship and instruction.

The longer a Christian lives his life apart from God, the more telling all these losses become. The solemn fact remains that, even after repentance, we cannot turn back the clock and relive those wasted years. It is well for the obedient Christian to recall these facts, since no amount of rejoicing about a brother's return can erase that brother's losses.

The father's final words are: "It was right that we should make merry and be glad, for your brother was dead and is alive again, and was lost and is found" (v 32). The words "it was right" translate a Greek verb that could also be rendered, "it was necessary." The father is arguing that in the very nature of the situation joy is fully appropriate. "For *your brother,*" says the father, was as good as dead to you; you had lost him. But now "your brother" is "alive" and "found"—that is, he is once again a part of your experience. That this is an appeal to brotherly affection hardly needs to be said.

Harmony with God

In fact, in referring to his brother, the older boy had called him *"this son of yours"!* And he had roundly condemned him because he had "devoured your livelihood *with harlots"* (v 30; italics added). But how did he know for sure about the harlots? He hadn't even talked to his brother yet! His spirit towards this erring brother is harshly judgmental. He thinks the very worst of him and is utterly lacking in brotherly affection. He won't even call him "my brother"! His father's words, *"your brother,"* gently remind him of this basic fact.

What the older brother sadly lacked was the perfectly natural feeling of joy that should come—not simply from recovering a son—but from recovering *a brother* as well. In the parable itself, this was in fact his *only* brother. How happy he should have been to see this *brother* walk back into his life, just as his father was so happy to see his *son* walk back into his. Joy was, after all, the truly natural reaction for both of them to such an event as this!

We Should Share Our Father's Joy

The apostle John has reminded us that "this commandment we have from Him: that he who loves God must love his brother also" (1 Jn 4:21). And he goes on immediately to say: "Whoever believes that Jesus is the Christ is born of God, and everyone who

The Self-Righteous Older Brother

loves Him who begot also loves him who is begotten of Him" (5:1). If a Christian truly loves his heavenly Father, he will also love his Christian brother, whom he recognizes as such—not by his obedient life—but by his faith in Christ for eternal life.

If love for the divine Begetter and His begotten child exist in the believer's heart, he will naturally experience joy when a wayward brother returns to God's flock. And in experiencing that joy he will "enter into" the very joy of God Himself. Or in other words, he will join the party!

The story of the self-righteous brother of the prodigal son carries a salutary reminder. Even those who remain in the Christian fellowship can get so out of touch with God's heart that they miss God's "feast of joy" when a backslider returns to the fold. But the same gracious Father who welcomes his prodigal sons and daughters home, also urges his self-righteous children to soften their hearts and join in the celebration.

—7—

UNLESS YOU REPENT: REPENTANCE IN LUKE 13:1-5

As we have seen in our previous chapters, biblical repentance is not a condition for eternal salvation. Instead it addresses the need that sinners have (whether saved or unsaved) to repair their relationship to God in order to prevent, or to terminate, His temporal judgment on their sins.

The prodigal son, for example, found himself in dire straits in the far country (Lk 15:14-16), and his miserable condition prompted his repentance which led to his reunion with his father (15:17-21). He is a classic example of a Christian backslider who responds to the discipline of God in his life and returns to fellowship with his heavenly Father.

Repentance and the Unsaved

But the call to repentance can also be addressed to an unsaved audience who is either experiencing, or about to experience, the temporal judgment of God upon their sins. Perhaps the classic biblical example of

Harmony with God

this is the case of Nineveh, recorded in the book of Jonah. So far as the statements of that book are concerned, the issue was God's temporal judgment: "Yet forty days, and Nineveh shall be overthrown" (Jonah 3:4).

Nineveh's repentance was impressive, to say the least, and involved everyone in the city, since this was commanded by "the king and his nobles" (3:7ff). There is not a word in the book of Jonah about the eternal salvation of the Ninevites, still less is there any suggestion that God's favor to them on this occasion was based on His free grace. On the contrary, the book of Jonah declares unmistakably: "Then God saw *their works*, that they turned from their evil way; and God relented from the disaster that He had said He would bring upon them, and He did not do it" (3:10, italics added).

None of this is contradicted, of course, by the statement of Jonah 3:5 that the Ninevites "believed God." As the context shows, they were believing the divine message proclaimed by Jonah: "Yet forty days and Ninevah shall be overthrown" (3:4).

When we come to the NT we discover that the doctrine of repentance is no different there than in the OT. In fact, both the preaching of John the Baptist and of our Lord Himself takes the OT doctrine for granted. Only when we realize this

Unless You Repent

simple, but obvious, fact can we read a number of NT passages with clarity and precision.

The Warning of Luke 13:1-5

Such a passage is found in Luke 13:1-5. On the occasion described there, the Lord Jesus is informed (though of course He already knew) about "the Galileans whose blood Pilate had mingled with their sacrifices" (13:1). The Roman governor had evidently executed certain persons from Galilee, quite possibly in the Temple itself where they had come to offer sacrifices to God. A ruthless act of this kind is completely consistent with the known character of this infamous Roman official.

Our Lord's response to this is striking. So far from expressing outrage at the governor's action, He takes it for granted that the disaster had occurred as a result of the sinfulness of those who had been killed. His words are a transparent appeal to all those listening to him to turn from their sins to God, for He says, "'Do you suppose that these Galileans were worse sinners than all other Galileans, because they suffered such things? I tell you, no; but unless you repent *you will all likewise perish*'" (13:2-3, italics added).

This statement by our Lord is immediately

Harmony with God

followed by another statement, which also refers to a temporal calamity. Jesus says, "Or those eighteen on whom the tower in Siloam fell and killed them, do you think that they were worse sinners than all other men who dwelt at Jerusalem? I tell you, no; but unless you repent *you will all likewise perish*" (13:4-5, italics added). Here too there is an evident appeal to turn from sin to God in order to avoid His temporal judgment.

We say that this is evident, but the point is sometimes overlooked. The word "perish," used in vv 3 and 5, has sometimes suggested to readers a reference to eternal judgment (as, e.g., in Jn 3:16). But the Greek word employed here (*apollumi*) could mean simply "to die" in normal Greek usage and was in fact freely used in the language in that sense. The context of our Lord's statements here shows plainly that this is how He was using it on this occasion. The Galileans and the men on whom the tower of Siloam had fallen had all *died*. Unless the audience repented, they too faced the prospect of physical death.

Moreover, the cases cited by Jesus suggest a calamitous death.

The Tragedy of 66-70 AD

There is no reason to doubt that the Lord is referring here to the impending tragedy for the nation which came to pass in the Jewish war with Rome in the years

Unless You Repent

AD 66-70. Pilate's brutality to the Galileans was but a faint "foretaste" of the thousands upon thousands of deaths that this war would bring. Josephus, the 1st century Jewish historian, places the number who died at 1,100,000, primarily Jews (*The Jewish War*, VI. 420-21).

The collapse of the tower of Siloam was likewise a mere shadow of the destruction that awaited the city of Jerusalem in that war. Our Lord and Savior stands here as a prophet greater than Jonah who foretells the divine wrath which must fall *unless Israel repents!* His

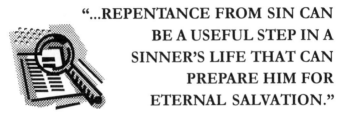

> "...REPENTANCE FROM SIN CAN BE A USEFUL STEP IN A SINNER'S LIFE THAT CAN PREPARE HIM FOR ETERNAL SALVATION."

words are focused on *temporal judgment!*

Repentance Can Prepare for Faith

To be sure, a repentant attitude on the part of Israel could prepare them to exercise faith in Christ for eternal life. This had indeed been the goal of John the Baptist's preaching, just as Paul states in Acts: "John indeed baptized with a baptism of repentance, saying to the people that they should believe on Him who would come after him, that is, on Christ Jesus" (Acts 19:4).

Harmony with God

But repentance itself was related to the need of the nation to avoid the calamities of AD 66-70 toward which its sinfulness was driving it.

It follows from what we are saying that repentance from sin can be a useful step in a sinner's life that can prepare him for eternal salvation. If the repentance toward God is genuine, then the heart is potentially open and responsive to a message of grace. In this sense, John's ministry was one of preparation for faith in Christ, precisely as Paul says it was.

Other Preparations for Faith

But it is equally true that other things may prepare us to be receptive to grace as well. In John 4, where repentance is not referred to at all, it was the frustrating emptiness of the Samaritan woman's pursuit of satisfaction that made her a ready candidate for the water of life. In John 9, it was the blind man's release from his lifelong disability that prepared his heart for faith in Christ. Here too there is no mention of repentance.

God has many ways of bringing men to Himself. Deep soul-thirst, or a sense of gratitude for some mercy of God, or repentance from sin are three obvious ways in which men are drawn to faith in Christ for eternal life. But none of these "routes" to faith should be mistaken for a "condition" for eternal life. Faith itself remains the one and only condition for that absolutely free gift.

Ready to Believe

It is often overlooked that the Philippian jailer was prepared for the saving message of Paul by the wonderful mercy of God in keeping all the prisoners in the jail and thereby preventing him from taking his own life. Paul has no need to speak to this man about repentance, for his question ("What must I do to be saved?") shows he is ready to believe (see Acts 16:27-31).

And when a man or woman is ready to hear the message of grace—no matter how God has worked to prepare them for that—then there is no need to speak to him or her at that point about repentance. Instead one may simply say, "Believe on the Lord Jesus Christ, and you will be saved" (Acts 16:31)!

—8—

REPENTANCE AND THE DAY OF THE LORD: 2 PETER 3:9

So far we have reached two fundamental conclusions about repentance. These are: (1) that repentance is not in any way a condition for eternal salvation; and (2) repentance is the decision to turn from sin to avoid, or bring to an end, God's temporal judgment. All the statements about repentance by the inspired writers of Scripture are consistent with these two basic principles, whether or not the repenting party or parties are saved or unsaved.

With this in mind, we can get a fresh perspective on a famous text related to the consummation of this age.

The Devastating Tribulation

In 2 Peter 3, the apostle is addressing the issue of the delay of our Lord's Second Advent. He notes that "scoffers will come in the last days" who make light of the Second Coming by saying, "Where is the promise

Harmony with God

of His coming? For since the fathers fell asleep, all things continue as they were from the beginning of creation" (2 Pet 3:3 and 4).

As part of his reply to this, Peter points to the flood of Noah's day by which "the world that then existed perished, being flooded with water" (v 6). This allusion to the flood carries us back to Jesus' words in the Olivet Discourse, where He states:

> But as the days of Noah were, so also will the coming of the Son of Man be. For as in the days before the flood, they were eating and drinking, marrying and giving in marriage, until the day that Noah entered the ark, and did not know until the flood came and took them all away, so also will the coming of the Son of Man be (Mt 24:38-39).

As is plain from these words, the Second Coming will be attended by devastating judgments comparable in scale to the flood of Noah's day.

This same point is made by Paul in 1 Thessalonians 5:2-3:

> For you yourselves know perfectly that the day of the Lord so comes as a thief in the night. For when they say, "Peace and safety!" then sudden destruction comes upon them, as labor pains upon a pregnant woman. And they shall not escape.

Besides this passage just quoted, it so happens that 2 Peter 3:10 is the only other NT text to affirm that "the day of the Lord will come as a thief in the night." Thus

Repentance and the Day of the Lord

Matthew 24, 1 Thessalonians 5 and 2 Peter 3 all agree that the eschatological period in view arrives at a time when normal life on earth has not been disrupted and that it occurs as a surprise to the world as unexpected as the arrival of a thief.

Among other things, this shows clearly that none of the devastating judgments that belong to the

> "...REPENTANCE IS THE DECISION TO TURN FROM SIN TO AVOID, OR BRING TO AN END, GOD'S TEMPORAL JUDGMENT."

Tribulation period have occurred prior to the day of the Lord. I have argued in my book, *Power to Make War* (Dallas: Redención Viva, 1995), that the "two witnesses" described in Revelation 11:3-13 carry on their ministry during the first 3 ½ years of Daniel's 70th week and that the judgments of God on the earth begin immediately at the commencement of this period (see pp. 46-50 of that book). Thus the advent of the day of the Lord must be placed no later than the beginning of Daniel's 70th week. Therefore, even within the initial 3 ½ years of this period, it is plain that the judgments will cause literally billions of deaths (see pp. 85-90 of *Power to Make War*).

Harmony with God

The Compassion of God.

This grave and solemn fact prepares us to appreciate the real thrust of Peter's argument here. His point is that the delay of the Second Coming is due to God's compassion for a world that will be swept by an almost incomprehensible number of deaths. Therefore, in 2 Peter 3:9 the apostle speaks as follows:

> The Lord is not slack concerning His promise, as some count slackness, but is longsuffering toward us, not willing that any should perish but that all should come to repentance.

There is no reference here to anyone's eternal destiny, although of course most of those who die under the judgments of the Tribulation will be unsaved. But the assertion about God's longsuffering is simply a statement about God's compassion toward sinful humanity. God would much prefer that "all" people in this sinful world should turn to Him in repentance, than that their unrepentant state should require—at last—the outpouring of the dreadful final judgments of this age. He therefore "tarries" in order to extend to mankind still further opportunity to repent of their sins. He really does not want anyone to "perish" (that is, to die) under these judgments.

As we have previously seen in our study of Luke 13:1-5, the word "perish" (Greek = *apollumi*) is a

Repentance and the Day of the Lord

perfectly good word to describe physical death. We need not invest it here with any other meaning than that. The fact is that the principle articulated by Peter in this text is also clearly stated in the Old Testament. Thus in Ezekiel, we hear God saying:

> "But if a wicked man turns from all his sins which he has committed, keeps all my statutes, and does what is lawful and right, he shall surely live; he shall not die ... Do I have any pleasure at all that the wicked should die?" says the Lord God, "and not that he should turn from his ways and live?" (Ezekiel 18:21, 23).

> "Repent, and turn from all your transgressions, so that iniquity will not be your ruin. Cast away from you all the transgressions which you have committed, and get yourselves a new heart and a new spirit. For why should you die, O house of Israel? For I have no pleasure in the death of one who dies," says the Lord God. "Therefore turn and live" (Ezekiel 18:30b-32).

Clearly in these passages from Ezekiel, the issue is one of life or death, in which it is evident that repentance followed by obedience (= "the fruits of repentance") can avert physical death and extend physical life. A compassionate God is never anxious to deliver sinners to their death, no matter how wicked they are. Thus, says Peter, He graciously delays the advent of the Day of the Lord, extending sinful man's opportunity to repent and avoid the judgment of death. The same doctrine that Peter teaches in 2 Peter 3:9 is

Harmony with God

taught as well by Paul in Romans 2:4-5. Indeed, Peter no doubt has Paul's teaching in mind (see 2 Pet 3:15).

Repentance Could Lead to Salvation

Of course, when sinners turn away from their sins to God, they are in a responsive mood toward the Lord and may well go on to salvation. But it would be a serious mistake to mix up the grounds for obtaining God's mercy that extends physical life with the grounds for obtaining eternal salvation.

Eternal salvation is always conditioned on faith alone and does not depend on how much or how little a sinner may have repented of his sins. To introduce repentance as an essential precursor to saving faith is false theology. Despite the efforts sometimes made to avoid saying so, if repentance from sin is an essential precursor to salvation, it is also a separate condition in addition to faith. Some forms of theology try to collapse repentance into a redefinition of faith (as though it was "included" in faith), but this is a theological undertaking for which there is not a shred of support in Scripture.

God therefore does not want anyone to die under the judgments of the Tribulation. If mankind were to repent and turn from their sins to Him, they could avert the devastating consequences that the end-times will

Repentance and the Day of the Lord

bring. Of course, knowing mankind, even a worldwide repentance would undoubtedly fade with time, and the eschatological judgments would finally come. Nineveh, for example, repented in Jonah's day and was spared, but ultimately it perished under God's wrath as the prophet Nahum correctly foretold.

Finally, were there to be a worldwide repentance sufficient in scope to postpone the eschatological day of temporal wrath, such a situation would be an excellent climate in which to preach the Gospel of God's saving grace. And no doubt there would be multitudes of converts. But even so, not even one of these converts would be saved by their repentance, but every single individual would be saved by faith alone in Christ alone!

—9—

NEW BIRTH, FORGIVENESS AND REPENTANCE

According to Luke 24:47, our Lord commanded that "repentance and remission [forgiveness] of sins should be preached in His name to all nations, beginning at Jerusalem." This mandate is definitely carried out in the book of Acts, as is made clear by Acts 2:38; 3:19; 5:31; and 8:22 in which both topics—repentance and forgiveness—are mentioned together.

In addition, repentance by itself is mentioned in Acts 11:18; 13:24; 17:30; 19:4; 20:21; and 26:20. Forgiveness by itself occurs in Acts 10:43; 13:38; and 26:18. It will be noted that the last two references (Acts 13:38 and 26:18) are quite close to two references to repentance (Acts 13:24 and 26:20). Repentance and forgiveness are quite closely tied in the book of Acts, a fact which conforms to the mandate our Lord gave in Luke 24:47.

What are we to make of this interesting connection?

Harmony with God

The Silence of the Fourth Gospel

We have already noted that the Gospel of John is completely silent about the subject of repentance (see the discussion in chapter 2). But it is often overlooked that the Fourth Gospel is almost equally silent about *forgiveness*.

I say *almost*, because there is one reference to forgiveness in John's Gospel, and it is found in John 20:23. In the statement made there, Jesus is speaking to the apostles after His resurrection and He says, "If you forgive the sins of any, they are forgiven them; if you retain the sins of any, they are retained."

Obviously, whatever this text means (and we will return to it in a later chapter), it *does not plainly declare* that forgiveness of sins is received by faith alone. And since John 20:23 is the only reference, we may also say that nowhere in John's Gospel is forgiveness of sins ever offered on the basis of faith alone. But by contrast, eternal life is offered on that basis *over and over again!*

Let us therefore restate what is obvious from these facts: (1) John is not interested in the subject of forgiveness in his Gospel apart from the one unusual passage referred to above; and (2) he is not interested at all in the subject of repentance. Of course, he *was* interested in these subjects as such,

New Birth, Forgiveness, and Repentance

but not for the purpose for which he wrote his Gospel. That purpose was to bring people to faith and eternal life (Jn 20:30-31).

We might therefore legitimately conclude from this that in terms of man's eternal destiny, the real issue is *not forgiveness but eternal life*. This inference is confirmed by John's own description of the Final Judgment of the lost in Revelation 20:11-14.

The Final Judgment

In John's well-known description of the Final Judgment, we do not even find a reference to sins, much less a reference to unforgiven sins. Instead, we are told, "the dead were judged according to their *works*, by the things which were written in the books" (Rev 20:12; italics added). To be sure, the works of unsaved people contain innumerable sins, but it is still significant that sin per se is not referred to, as we will point out in a moment.

Yet even though unsaved people are judged on the basis of their works, *they are not condemned to hell on that basis!* On the contrary we read, "And anyone not found written in *the Book of Life* was cast into the lake of fire" (Rev 20:15; italics added). People go to hell, therefore, because they do not have *life!*

This is precisely what we might have concluded

Harmony with God

from the theme statement of the Fourth Gospel: "but these are written that you may believe that Jesus is the Christ, the Son of God, and that believing you may have *life* in His name" (Jn 20:31; italics added). It is also evident in John 5:24 where our Lord states that the believer "shall not come into *judgment*, but has passed from death into *life*" (italics added). We conclude, therefore, that the possession of *life* is the critical issue between God and man in terms of eternal judgment. There is *no Final Judgment* to determine one's eternal destiny if he already possesses *life*.

But sin is *not the critical issue*. Why not? John's own writings tell us why. According to John, Jesus is "the Lamb of God who takes away the sin of the world" (John 1:29); and "He Himself is the propitiation for our sins, and not for ours only but also for the whole world" (1 Jn 2:2). The hymn writer was correct when he said that "Jesus paid it all"!

So marvelously complete and full is the sacrificial death of Christ for our sins that God's justice is satisfied by that sacrifice and no man is condemned to hell on the grounds of his sins. But by the same token, the cross of Christ does not automatically regenerate men and women. They still need to obtain *life* and this is available to them on one basis only: *faith in Christ*.

New Birth, Forgiveness, and Repentance

But then, one might ask, why do men's works come up at all? The reason must surely be that at the Final Judgment mankind will get a full and fair hearing. Since multitudes have supposed that they can reach heaven by their works, these works will be examined on that day. But as Scripture already informs us, no man can be saved by his works (Eph 2:8-9; Tit 3:5; Rom 3:20).

The outcome of the final examination of the works of the lost is a foregone conclusion. Any claim to God's salvation that is based on the deeds a person has done will be swept away by the contents of the books that are opened at the judgment. Man's one last hope will rest in the Book of Life, which will be duly consulted even though those being judged do not have their names written there. But the absence of their names from its pages is the basis on which the lost are cast into the lake of fire.

Thus one can see that the issue at the Final Judgment is not man's *sin*, since Christ has atoned for that in its entirety. Instead, the issue is whether someone can make it into the kingdom of God on the basis of the works they did on earth, apart from the miracle of new birth that comes by faith alone. But as the Lord Jesus informed Nicodemus, "Most assuredly, I say to you, unless one is born again, he cannot see the kingdom of God" (Jn 3:3).

Harmony with God

Forgiveness and Final Judgment

It should be carefully noted, however, that we have certainly not said that man's sins are *already forgiven* on the basis of the cross. To say so would be to fly into the face of many Scriptures. But the question arises, how can this *not* be so if in fact Christ

> "MOST CHRISTIANS TEND TO PLACE ETERNAL LIFE AND FORGIVENESS OF SINS IN THE SAME CATEGORY. BUT THIS IS A SERIOUS MISTAKE."

has already atoned for the sins of all humanity? This is a good question that deserves our attention.

What is involved here is what may be described as a "category error." Most Christians tend to place eternal life and forgiveness of sins into the same category. But this is a serious mistake.

It is not at all hard to see how the propitiation Christ made on the cross can satisfy God's righteous judgment without automatically imparting eternal life to the unsaved person. Satisfaction for sin and the impartation of eternal life to a dead sinner are clearly separate and distinguishable actions.

New Birth, Forgiveness, and Repentance

But for most Christians, an unforgiven sin means a sin not paid for, and therefore *it seems to follow* that if all sin has been paid for, it should all be automatically forgiven. But this line of reasoning is deeply flawed and unbiblical.

Its first and foremost flaw is this: *all sin IS paid for!* But if that is true, forgiveness *cannot be* the remission of some unpaid penalty. In the same way, unforgiven sin *cannot be* sin for which *we must pay as well as Christ. That would be double payment,* and it would call into question the efficacy of the cross.

Let us emphasize this point. The Lord Jesus Christ is not just *potentially* the propitiation for the sins of the world. He IS that (1 Jn 2:2). Or as Paul puts it, "God was in Christ reconciling *the world* to Himself, not imputing their trespasses to them" (2 Cor 5:19; italics added). From the standpoint of God's righteous demands as the Judge of all humanity, all humanity's sin was paid for by Christ and none of it remains as an issue in man's final judgment. None of it! Not one single bit!

We must conclude, therefore, that forgiveness is also not an issue at the Final Judgment. People *do* go to hell unforgiven, but they do not go to hell *because* they are unforgiven. Just as sin itself is not an issue at the Final Judgment, neither is forgiveness

Harmony with God

an issue there.

What Is Forgiveness?

What then is forgiveness? Let us now make a simple statement: *Forgiveness is not a judicial issue between man and God, but a personal issue between man and God.*

An illustration may help here. Suppose I go to court on charges of stealing someone's car. The judge before whom I stand does not concern himself with the issue of forgiveness. As a judge, his only concern is with the question of guilt or innocence. He will either clear me or condemn me.

But suppose it was the judge's car that I stole? As an individual he can choose to forgive me, or not to forgive me. But whether he does or not, the decision has nothing to do with his role as a judge. It is purely a personal matter between myself and him.

In the Bible, forgiveness is always a personal matter—whether between man and man or between man and God. Let us consider the interesting passage in Luke 17:3-4 where we read:

> Take heed to yourselves. If your brother sins against you, rebuke him; and if he repents, forgive him. And if he sins against you seven times in a day, and seven times in a day returns to you, saying, "I repent," you shall forgive him.

New Birth, Forgiveness, and Repentance

Here it is quite evident that there is no issue of "penalty" in the legal or judicial sense of that word. The issue is purely one of *personal harmony* between the offended party and the offender. That harmony has been disrupted by one brother's sin against another, and upon the offending brother's repentance harmony can be restored by the offended brother extending forgiveness.

There is nothing mysterious about the process just described. All of us understand it instinctively in human relationships. We are not judges sitting in a courtroom and issuing judicial edicts against our sinning brothers. We may indeed exact a *personal penalty* from our sinning brother. This may take the form of refusing to speak to him, refusing to socialize, cutting off financial or other support, or any number of other things—but all of these are personal actions, not legal decisions.

The same is true in man's dealings with God. At the level of *personal harmony* with God, forgiveness repairs the rupture caused by sin. Someone has said, appropriately, that forgiveness removes the *estrangement between God and man* which man's sin has caused.

Yet as we all know, truly born again people can become estranged from God by pursuing a sinful

Harmony with God

path. But when they *repent* and return to God (as the Prodigal Son returned to his father), they are *forgiven* and their harmony with God is restored. The father of the Prodigal Sin forgave his repentant boy and the two went into the house and had a joyous party together!

Conclusion

Repentance and forgiveness of sins, therefore, are not issues in the Final Judgment of mankind. Sin itself, as such, is not an issue either, because Jesus' death on the cross completely satisfied every judicial demand that God had in connection with man's sin.

But the cross does not automatically regenerate men. It does, however, *make regeneration possible*. In the same way, since God's judicial demands against sin have been met, the cross makes possible the repair of the *personal barrier* between sinful men and a holy God. If that barrier is to be repaired, if harmony is to be restored between the wayward sinner and his Maker, the straying sinner is called upon to repent and to seek forgiveness. When forgiveness is received, God and man can have fellowship with each other.

The forgiven man is not only saved from eternal

New Birth, Forgiveness, and Repentance

hell. He is in personal harmony with his God.

—10—

HARMONY WITH GOD

We are now ready to make a new statement about repentance. Repentance is indeed a decision to turn from sin in order to avoid, or put an end to, God's temporal judgment. But we can also say this: *Repentance can and should lead to harmony with God.*

Of course, this is an obvious lesson in the classic story of the Prodigal Son. This son's repentance occurred in the far country, but it led him back to his father and finally into the splendid reunion party which they enjoyed together. The Prodigal Son had done more than escape from the woeful conditions (=chastening) into which his sin had led him. He was now *in harmony* with his father, from whom he had so long been separated.

But the father of the Prodigal Son also had a specific role in this restoration of harmony between himself and his son. What did the father do? He *forgave*, and he *forgave* completely, generously and without reserve. He forgave the way God forgives!

Harmony with God

Let us think about these issues in somewhat more detail.

Repentance and Remission of Sins

As we noted in the previous chapter, after His resurrection our Lord and Savior announced to His disciples that "repentance and remission [forgiveness] of sins should be preached in His name to all nations" (Lk 24:47). What message is this? Basically it is a call to the people of all nations to find *harmony with God* through Jesus Christ.

How does man's eternal salvation relate to this message? Very simply: *God will not forgive the sins of those who are still unsaved.* God cannot have true harmony with the unsaved.

This is different, of course, than putting an end to His temporal judgments. Let us here remember the Ninevites. They *repented* and, as a result, "God saw their works, that they turned from their evil way; and *God relented* from the evil that he had said that He would bring upon them, and He did not do it" (Jonah 3:10). There is not a syllable here about *forgiveness*. All we are told is that God rescinded the pronouncement that Ninevah would be overthrown in forty days (see Jonah 3:4).

Did any of the Ninevites get saved? We are not

Harmony with God

told. Yet it is evident that by sparing the city God gave the Ninevites a renewed opportunity to come to know Him. It seems highly probable that many of them *did* get saved (cf. Mt 12:41; Lk 11:32), but if they did they needed more information than is recorded in the book of Jonah. Of course, it is quite possible that Jonah gave them such information, but if so this has no role in the subject matter of Jonah's book.

And equally, neither is *forgiveness* part of Jonah's

> **"...REPENTANCE AND FORGIVENESS OF SINS ARE RELATED TO EACH OTHER BUT THEY ARE STILL SEPARATE CONSIDERATIONS. REPENTANCE MOVES MAN *IN THE DIRECTION OF* FORGIVENESS."**

subject matter. We really do not know how many, if any, of the inhabitants of that city found *harmony with God*. All we know is that for the time being their city was not destroyed, although later on it *was* destroyed as the prophet Nahum predicted. *Forgiveness* is not an issue in Jonah.

Of similar significance is our Lord's treatment of the *potential repentance* of Tyre and Sidon, as well as of Sodom. In the case of Sodom it is even stated

Harmony with God

that if it had repented it would have "remained until this day," that is, its destruction would have been averted (Mt 11:20-24; see also Lk 10:13-14). The Son of God thus knew an "alternate history" for Sodom right down to His own time, had that city repented. But these texts do not discuss the eternal salvation of the citizens of the cities in question.

Thus repentance and remission (forgiveness) of sins are related to each other, but they are still separate considerations. Repentance moves man (as it did the Prodigal Son) *in the direction of* forgiveness.

Forgiveness for Cornelius

Unlike the book of Jonah, in the book of Acts forgiveness is very much an issue. Indeed, the classic case of forgiveness for Gentiles is nothing less than the famous story about Cornelius, the Roman centurion.

Cornelius was clearly a man who *repented* well before his conversion to Christ. This is manifest from the fact that we are told that he was "a devout man and one who feared God with all his household, who gave alms generously to the people, and prayed to God always" (Acts 10:2).

Let us remember that Cornelius was a pagan Gentile, but obviously at some point in time he had

Harmony with God

turned away from his paganism in order to seek the God of Israel. He did this, in fact, with a diligence that might well have put many a Jewish person to shame. Thus he was ready for the message of the Gospel, which however he *still needed to hear*.

This is where Peter comes in. This great Apostle was to be God's messenger to Cornelius to show him how *to be saved* (see Acts 11:14). According to the angel's own words, therefore, the issue to be addressed by Peter would be the issue of his *salvation*.

The message Peter subsequently gives to Cornelius and to his assembled friends reaches its climax with these words: "And He [Christ] commanded us to preach to the people, and to testify that it is He who was ordained by God to be Judge of the living and the dead. To Him all the prophets witness that, through His name, whoever believes in Him will receive remission [forgiveness] of sins" (Acts 10:42-43).

The believing response by Cornelius and his friends was immediate (v 44). The *repentant* centurion now became the *forgiven* centurion. His repentance had led him to salvation and to *harmony* with God.

Cornelius, the Gentile Model

Harmony with God

Readers of the book of Acts often forget that the inspired author necessarily condenses his material and selects what he includes in accordance with his purposes in writing. The speech of Peter in the household of Cornelius (Acts 10:34-43) takes us less than two minutes to read aloud! Obviously, on this momentous occasion Peter did not speak for *less than two minutes*. The speech is highly compressed to bring out what Luke desires to bring out.

Did Luke himself think that Cornelius received eternal life on this occasion? Of course he did. That was a part of Luke's theology as is made clear in Acts 13:48 where he writes, "And as many as had been appointed to eternal life believed." Did Peter mention eternal life to his audience on this occasion? There is not a reason in the world why he should not have. But for Luke, the major point to be made is *forgiveness*.

Why? Well, for one thing, Luke's obvious purpose in telling the Cornelius narrative is to establish the fact that God has accepted believing Gentiles as fully as He has accepted believing Jews. This point is made when Peter defends himself at Jerusalem (Acts 11:4-17). Accordingly, *forgiveness* is stressed in the Cornelius story to highlight the fact that these Gentiles were completely accepted into God's fellowship. That they also had received eternal life

Harmony with God

Luke evidently expected his readers to know.

But if God had accepted them, the Jewish church must do so as well. If Gentiles were in fellowship with God, they could also be in fellowship with their Jewish brothers in Christ.

Cornelius thus stands before us in Luke's narrative as a classic case of Gentile conversion. Some time before Peter came to him, he had turned away from his paganism and that repentance had put him on the road to a saving encounter with the God of Israel. But the salvation he receives in Acts 10 is by simple faith, and not only does he receive eternal life, but also the forgiveness of sins and the gift of the Holy Spirit (Acts 10:43-44).

This is precisely what happens to all of us at the moment when we trust Christ for salvation. Cornelius is the model for our own experience of God's grace.

In Cornelius's case, repentance from his paganism prepared him for the moment of his conversion. So too, of course, many Gentiles in our own day and time turn to God from broken lives, or unsatisfying experiences, or false religious ideas, long before they come to understand God's saving grace. They may even start going to church, praying and reading their Bible. Thus, although repentance saves no one, it can prepare a person to receive the message of grace

Harmony with God

with openness—just as Cornelius did in Acts 10.

Repentance and Idol Worship

The story of the conversion of Cornelius helps us to understand another important text on repentance. This text is found in the account of Paul's speech on the Areopagus (Mars Hill) in the sophisticated pagan city of Athens (Acts 17:22-31).

As presented by Luke, Paul's speech on the Areopagus has as its central concern the paganism that was everywhere so evident in Athens. Indeed the speech is even a classic model of the biblical and Jewish case against idol worship. There is not so much as a word in this speech about sinful *practices*. Instead its focus is on sinful *worship*.

It is from this sinful worship—from idolatry—that Paul calls on his readers to repent. He declares: "Truly, these times of ignorance God overlooked, but now commands all men everywhere to *repent*, because He has appointed a day on which He will judge the world in righteousness by the Man whom He has ordained. He has given assurance of this to all by raising Him from the dead" (Acts 17:30-31; italics added).

Obviously, the pagan idolatry of Paul's hearers stood in the way of their turning to the true and

Harmony with God

living God in faith. No one who believed in the worship of images was properly prepared to accept the exclusive claims of the Creator and of His Son, Jesus Christ. According to Paul, the God he proclaimed was the Judge of all the world. Thus a man's eternal destiny was determined by the true and living God, not by any of the countless pagan deities that Athens honored with her idols.

Thus Paul's call for repentance from idolatry was intended to prepare his hearers to have dealings with the God who would "judge the world in righteousness."

Cornelius, as we have previously seen, had already given up his idolatry before Peter came to his house. He was ready for Peter's message. But where this readiness was not present—as it was not on the Areopagus—Paul's message must lay the groundwork for that by challenging his hearers to turn "to God from idols" (see 1 Thess 1:9).

Let us remember here too that the speech recorded in Acts 17:22-31 is the merest fragment of what Paul must have said on this occasion. That he must have mentioned faith in Christ is shown by the fact that "some men joined him and *believed*" (17:34; italics added). But Luke's purpose behind his record here is to show how Paul dealt with idolatry in the Gentile world. His purpose is *not* to give a complete account

Harmony with God

of all that Paul said.

Clearly we see here how repentance can prepare the way for faith. It is no different than when an unsaved person turns in disgust from a sinful lifestyle and looks for a relationship with God. Repentance does not save him, but it prepares him to come to faith.

Thus we can more accurately appreciate Paul's summary of his own preaching as the process of "testifying to Jews, and also to Greeks, *repentance* toward God and *faith* toward our Lord Jesus Christ" (Acts 20:21; italics added; see also Acts 26:20). As this statement plainly shows, repentance and faith are by no means synonymous. They are distinct issues.

Conclusion

Luke's treatment of the theme of repentance and forgiveness in connection with the Gentile mission has two significant aspects.

(1) Repentance from pagan idolatry is an important step toward faith wherever idolatry has created a barrier to coming to faith in Christ.

(2) Faith in Christ not only bestows eternal life on the Gentile believer but bestows forgiveness as well.

Thus, at the moment he believes in Christ, the

Harmony with God

Gentile believer enters into personal harmony with the God from whom he had been estranged.

—11—

REPENTANCE IN PALESTINE

Many of the New Testament references to repentance refer to the situation in Palestine during, and immediately following, the ministry of John the Baptist and of our Lord Jesus Christ. No discussion of repentance would be complete without considering these passages.

In the process of examining this class of passages, we will encounter some special historical situations that are crucial to completing our study on repentance. Even if they are not mentioned specifically, passages that are to be understood in the light of the following discussion are: Mt 3:2, 8, 11; 4:17; 9:13; Mk 1:4, 15; 2:17; 6:12; Lk 3:3, 8; 5:32; and Acts 5:31; 13:24.

Repentance and John the Baptist

We can hardly find a better summary of the ministry of John the Baptist than the one Paul gives in Acts 19:4. There he is addressing some disciples who seemed to lack the gift of the Spirit. His question to them had

Harmony with God

been: "Did you receive the Holy Spirit when you believed?" (Acts 19:2).

The disciples' reply can be translated, "We have not so much as heard if the Holy Spirit is *here*" (Acts 19:2; italics added). The words "is *here*" translate a Greek phrase that can be rendered simply "is." From this fact many have drawn the conclusion that these disciples of John the Baptist had no knowledge of the Third Person of the Trinity, i.e., they didn't know He existed.

This is highly improbable, since John the Baptist, whose disciples they were, preached about the Spirit (Mk 1:8 and other places). But a clue to the real meaning of the text here is found in John 7:39.

In that passage John explains a statement made by our Lord by saying, "But this He spoke concerning the Spirit, whom those believing in Him would receive; for the Holy Spirit was not yet *given* [supplied by NKJV], because Jesus was not yet glorified" (Jn 7:39). The literal rendering would be: "the Spirit was not yet"!

Both in Acts 19:4 and John 7:39, the coming of the Holy Spirit at Pentecost is described by a simple "to be" verb. Since the author of the Fourth Gospel was almost certainly originally a disciple of the Baptist (i.e., he is the unnamed disciple in Jn 1:35-40), we probably have here an expression used among the disciples of the Baptist. To say that "the Holy Spirit is not yet" or

Repentance in Palestine

"is" was to state that He had not yet come or had come. This alone makes real sense of Acts 19:2.

Once he has discovered that these men did *not yet possess* the gift of the Spirit, Paul asks a further question: "Into what then were you baptized?" (19:3). (That Paul should think of baptism here is a most interesting fact to which we will return later in the chapter.) The men reply, "Into John's baptism" (19:3).

As soon as Paul has ascertained that these disciples were John's disciples, he reminds them of the nature of John's ministry. His words are, "John indeed baptized with a baptism of repentance, saying to the people that they should believe on Him who would come after him, that is, on Christ Jesus" (Acts 19:4). The result of this explanation by Paul is that these men "were baptized in the name of the Lord Jesus" (19:5) and then—but only then—do they receive the Holy Spirit by the laying on of Paul's hands (19:6).

For the moment we must especially note the *preparatory nature* of John's ministry proclaiming repentance. It was designed to prepare "the people" for faith. Thus far, at least, this is consistent with what we have already learned about the relationship between repentance and faith.

The Fruits of Repentance

Harmony with God

Paul's summary of John's ministry is perfectly accurate. But the Gospels give us somewhat more detail. For one thing, they inform us that John called for the production of "fruits worthy of repentance" (Mt 3:8; Lk 3:8).

If we ask what these fruits were to be, the answer is perfectly clear in Luke 3:10-14 where, in response to a series of questions asking, "What shall we do?" (vv 10, 12, 14) the people, tax collectors and soldiers

> "IT IS ONE THING TO SAY THAT REPENTANCE *FACLITATES* FAITH IN CHRIST FOR ETERNAL LIFE—THE BIBLE TEACHES THAT. IT IS QUITE ANOTHER THING TO SAY THAT REPENTANCE IS A *REQUIREMENT* FOR ETERNAL LIFE. THAT THE BIBLE DOES *NOT* TEACH."

are all informed about the actions that constitute the fruit of repentance. Needless to say, had such actions been carried out on a wide scale the entire atmosphere in Israel would have been changed, and the nation would have been preparing itself for faith in the One coming after John.

Although the simple gospel of faith in Christ specifies no preconditions at all, the fact remains that

Repentance in Palestine

a repentant heart is obviously better soil for faith than an unrepentant one. It is one thing to say that repentance *facilitates* faith in Christ for eternal life—the Bible teaches that. It is quite another thing to say that repentance is a *requirement* for eternal life. That the Bible does *not* teach.

But even in the ministry of John the Baptist the theme of impending temporal judgment is a part of his message about repentance.

The Ax and the Fire

When John the Baptist exhorted his audience to "bear fruits worthy of repentance" (Mt 3:8; Lk 3:8), he warned them that "even now the ax is laid to the root of the trees. Therefore every tree which does not bear good fruit is cut down and thrown into the fire" (Mt 3:10; Lk 3:9). There is little reason to doubt that here John was speaking prophetically about the impending disaster that was to come on the nation of Israel during the calamitous war with Rome in 66-70 AD.

In the light of all we have seen about repentance up to now, there is nothing to commend the view that John is referring to the "fire" of eternal damnation. Fire is a frequent OT image of God's temporal wrath and there is no justification for not taking it that way

Harmony with God

here. See, for example, its repeated use in this way in Amos 1:4, 7, 10, 12, 14; 2:2, 5. (For the imagery of God's wrath as fire burning up trees, see Jer 21:12-14; 22:6-7; Eze 15:1-8 [the wood of the vine]; see also Isa 9:19; Jer 48:45; Hos 8:14; Nah 1:6; Zeph 1:18; the references could be multiplied.)

Clearly John's call to repentance accompanied by its fruits adheres firmly to the Bible's fundamental concept of repentance. By repenting sincerely so that the appropriate actions follow, human beings are invited to escape, or avoid, the temporal judgments of God. But such repentance can lead on to the experience of forgiveness of sin and harmony with God. This too was a part of John's message.

Baptism *for* Forgiveness

In two texts in the Gospels (Mk 1:4 and Lk 3:3) it is directly declared that John preached "a baptism of repentance *for* the remission [forgiveness] of sins." It is plain, therefore, that John's audience was being told that the baptism by which they expressed their repentance was a condition for the forgiveness of their sins.

In other words, they could not achieve harmony with God apart from receiving baptism. But it does not follow from this that forgiveness was bestowed at

Repentance in Palestine

once on all who were baptized—or even upon those who did this sincerely (in contrast to going along with the crowds). As we have already suggested, true harmony with God our Maker can only begin when we enter His family by way of new birth. Until then, the unsaved man is "dead in trespasses and sins" (Eph 2:1).

As we have seen, even Cornelius who had sincerely turned to God with actions that God acknowledged, did not have either peace or forgiveness before he believed in Christ (cf. Acts 10:36, 43). In the same way, we should conclude that just as John's baptism was intended to prepare men for faith in the Messiah who would soon appear, so also it prepared them to receive the forgiveness which only faith in Him could give.

But there was a difference from the experience of Cornelius. Cornelius received forgiveness *before* water baptism. The Jews of Palestine could not.

Palestine after the Cross

We need to recall that impressively large numbers of Israelites accepted John's baptism. Mark records that "*all* the land of Judea, and those from Jerusalem, went out to him and were *all* baptized by him in the Jordan River, confessing their sins" (Mk 1:5; italics added). Matthew and Luke refer as well to "*all* the region around

Harmony with God

the Jordan" (Mt 3:5, italics added; Lk 3:3). What amounted to a national revival appeared to be taking place.

But the spiritual movement begun by John eventually collapsed. True, many Israelites believed in the One John had proclaimed (and thus entered into harmony with God through forgiveness of sins), but many more did not. What had begun as a wave of national repentance was reversed over time into a national rejection of God's Christ, with the people loudly demanding that Jesus be crucified and invoking the dreadful curse, "His blood be on us and on our children" (Mt 27:25).

This tragic departure from an initial movement in the direction of faith in Christ and harmony with His heavenly Father left Israel more estranged than ever from her God. It is not at all incomprehensible that God should withhold the privilege of harmony with Himself until a repentant Israelite submitted to baptism in the name of His beloved Son, whom Israel had crucified. The evidence of the book of Acts points unmistakably to the conclusion that God insisted on this kind of baptism before He would forgive the sins of the believing Israelites or grant them the gift of the Holy Spirit.

Let it be clearly said that the simple way of eternal salvation was *not changed*, even for the Israelites of

Repentance in Palestine

Palestine. Eternal life is always received on the basis of faith alone in Christ alone. Thus the Judge of all mankind accepts the faith of any and every human being who believes in Christ for eternal life. No such person is in any danger at all of eternal damnation.

But *forgiveness*, as we have seen, is *personal and not judicial*. God may set whatever terms He wishes for the restoration of harmony with Himself. The evidence of Acts loudly proclaims the special conditions that obtained in Palestine immediately after the cross.

Baptism in Jesus' Name

The disciples of John whom Paul met in Acts 19 were obviously at one time residents of Palestine, since the ministry of John the Baptist was confined to that land. But equally obvious is the fact that though they had believed (Acts 19:2), this did not immediately confer on them the gift of the Holy Spirit. Among Palestinians, God was only bestowing the Holy Spirit on baptized believers.

Paul knew this, of course, and when he discerns that the twelve do not yet have the Spirit, he turns at once to the issue of baptism. And though these men *have been* baptized, their baptism was with "John's baptism" (Acts 19:3). Thereupon Paul proceeds to baptize them "in the name of the Lord Jesus" (Acts

Harmony with God

19:5), after which he "laid hands on them" and "the Holy Spirit came upon them" (Acts 19:6).

It is perfectly obvious that baptism in the name of Jesus is the issue here. For these men it had to *precede* the gift of the Spirit.

What we see in Acts 19 replicates what occurs in Samaria in Acts 8. The converts of Philip the evangelist receive the Holy Spirit only after baptism and only after

> **"THERE IS NO NEED TO ATTEMPT TO MAKE ACTS 2:38 SAY THE SAME THING AS JOHN 3:16; 5:24; 6:47; AND MANY OTHER VERSES. IT DOES *NOT SAY THE SAME THING!*"**

the apostles Peter and John come down to them, pray for them and bestow the Spirit on them exactly as Paul did to the twelve in Acts 19. The Samaritans too, of course, were Palestinians and had been exposed to the ministry of John and of the Lord Jesus Christ.

The same thing may be said of Acts 2:38, a verse widely misunderstood and misapplied. When the Pentecostal audience heard Jesus proclaimed as "both Lord and Christ" (Acts 2:36), they indicated their belief of this truth with the words, "Men and brethren, what shall we do?" (Acts 2:37). But to believe that Jesus is

Repentance in Palestine

the Christ is to be born again and possess eternal life (Jn 20:30-31; 1 Jn 5:1). Thus at this point the hearers who asked this question had been eternally saved!

What did they lack? They lacked *harmony with God,* whom they had so deeply offended. What did they need to do? Two things: "Repent, and let every one of you be baptized in the name of Jesus Christ" (Acts 2:38). What would happen if they did these things? The answer is that they would receive "remission (forgiveness) of sins" and "the gift of the Holy Spirit" (Acts 2:38).

There is no need here to attempt, as many have done, to make this famous verse (Acts 2:38) say the same thing as John 3:16; 5:24; 6:47; and many other verses. It does *not say the same thing!* Why not? Because eternal life and forgiveness of sins are *not the same thing! The former is required for eternal salvation, the latter for harmony with God.*

Paul, the Jewish Model

We have seen already that Cornelius is the classic model for Gentile salvation. He believes in Christ and immediately receives the forgiveness of sins and the Holy Spirit. Paul, however, is the model for the salvation of Palestinian Jews.

If we ask at what point Paul believed that Jesus

Harmony with God

was the Christ and received eternal life, there can be only one answer. It happened on the road to Damascus when the Risen Savior responded to Paul's question, "Who are you, Lord?" with this reply, "I am Jesus, whom you are persecuting" (Acts 9:5). There is no reason to doubt that Paul believed these words then and there and thus received eternal salvation (1 Jn 5:1).

But *not* forgiveness of sins. Indeed, it is only from his speech to the Jerusalem mob in Acts 22 that we actually learn when Paul was forgiven. It should be noted in regard to this speech that Paul is deliberately identifying with his Palestinian audience in order to draw them to faith in Christ (see Acts 22:3). His experience can be theirs as well. So it is only here that we discover some details of the visit of Ananias to Paul that are not given in Luke's other accounts of Paul's conversion (Acts 9 and 26).

In Acts 22 alone do we learn that Ananias said to Paul on that occasion, "And now why are you waiting? Arise and be baptized, and *wash away your sins*, calling on the name of the Lord" (Acts 22:16; italics added). Here we note once again the intimate connection between baptism and the forgiveness of sins for a Palestinian convert (even though he is in Damascus at this moment!). That Paul also received the Holy Spirit at this time is indirectly suggested by Acts 9:17. Thus Paul's own experience of conversion fundamentally

Repentance in Palestine

reproduces the sequence found in Acts 2:36-38.

Paul's total conversion experience, therefore, is the model for the conversion of Palestinian Jews: that is,

(1) Faith for eternal life and
(2) Baptism for the forgiveness of sins, followed by
(3) The gift of the Holy Spirit.

Cornelius on the other hand is the Gentile model:

(1) Faith immediately bringing eternal life, forgiveness of sins, and the gift of the Holy Spirit, followed by
(2) Water baptism.

When these sequences are kept in mind, the confusion many have felt about certain statements in Acts is removed. For Cornelius, repentance preceded the whole process though it was not a condition for salvation. For Paul, as for all Palestinians, repentance preceded forgiveness and *was* a condition for that, though not for eternal salvation.

Of course, the text of Acts 22 does not specifically indicate exactly when Paul repented. But this could hardly have occurred before he got an answer to his question, "Who are You, Lord?" Only after the reply, "I am Jesus of Nazareth, whom you are persecuting" (Acts 22:8) could he have had the information needed for repentance. So here, clearly, belief that the glorified

Harmony with God

Jesus was the Christ necessarily preceded his repentance. This parallels the faith implicitly expressed in Acts 2:37, which precedes the call to repentance in Acts 2:38.

The parallelism between Paul's experience and that of the converts of Acts 2 is thus very precise.

The Gift of the Holy Spirit

Receiving the gift of the Holy Spirit, of course, is not identical with being born again by the Spirit. New birth has always been a condition for entrance into the kingdom of God (Jn 3:3), but the gift of the Spirit, which creates our union with the spiritual body of Christ (1 Cor 12:13), has only been given since Pentecost (Jn 7:39). Old Testament saints did not have such a union with Christ, which results from the Spirit's baptizing work, accomplished at the same time He comes to indwell us (see the contrast between "with you" and "in you" in John 14:17).

The gift of the Spirit, of course, is not merited in any way by any act or deed. What could earn us such a gift? But in Acts this special gift was only bestowed on those who obtained harmony with God through the forgiveness of sins. This is true of Gentiles and Jews alike, though with Gentiles it is simultaneous with everything else the believer gets at the moment of faith.

Repentance in Palestine

Eternal life is a free gift given to all who believe. The gift of the Spirit is God's gift to that circle of people that is in harmony with Himself. It is like the man who goes out at the Christmas season to buy gifts for all his friends. The fact that he does not also buy gifts for everyone in his neighborhood does not make his presents for his friends anything less than free gifts.

Eternal life is God's *universal* gift, offered to all humanity on the basis of faith alone. The gift of the Holy Spirit is His *restricted* gift, given to all who have come into harmony with Himself by means of the forgiveness of sins.

In the Palestinian situation that followed the crucifixion of our Lord Jesus Christ, God insisted that Palestinian Jews who were exposed to the baptizing witness of John should receive baptism in Jesus' name. If they were already believers, like the twelve men of Acts 19 (see v 2), they needed baptism only to place themselves in a position to receive the Spirit.

Presumably these twelve men had received both eternal life and forgiveness of sins before they encountered Paul. Paul says nothing to them about either of these things. The sole question is whether they possessed the gift of the Spirit, and for this they needed baptism in the name of Jesus Christ.

This suggests that they are examples of sincere disciples of the Baptist who followed through on their

Harmony with God

baptism by John to subsequently believe in "Him who would come after him, that is, on Jesus Christ" (Acts 19:4 with 19:2). But they had not been baptized in the name of Jesus as yet, perhaps because they had left Palestine before Pentecost to come (for reasons unknown to us) to the Roman province of Asia, where Paul finds them.

Thus they are somewhat different from typical Palestinian converts, such as those in Acts 2 or Paul. Their own experience might be laid out in the following steps:

(1) Baptism by John,
(2) Subsequent faith in Christ by which they received eternal life and forgiveness of sins,
(3) Baptism by Paul in the name of Jesus Christ, and
(4) Receiving the gift of the Spirit through the laying on of Paul's hands.

It is certainly worth noting here that though baptism in Christ's name was a prerequisite, it did not automatically confer on them the gift of the Spirit. The same is true of the Samaritans in Acts 8 (see 8:14-17). Baptism simply admitted them into the closed circle upon whom God was willing to bestow His Spirit. But this separation between baptism and the gift of the Spirit (in that the former does not automatically confer the latter) is a good reminder that this great gift, like

Repentance in Palestine

eternal life, is completely unmerited.

Conclusion

Like Cornelius, our experience of salvation is basically simple and full. All of the spiritual benefits that every believer needs are bestowed at once at the moment of faith. When a person believes in Christ he receives: (1) eternal life by means of the new birth, (2) forgiveness of sins (so that harmony with God may begin), and (3) the gift of the Spirit.

We should mention as well that at the moment of faith we are also *justified*, that is, we are cleared of every charge of sin and granted a perfect righteousness before the bar of God's justice (see Rom 3:21-26: 5:1; 8:31-34). There is much that could be said about this great theme (which lies at the heart of the book of Romans), but this is not the place to say it. Suffice it to observe that every justified believer is born again, and every born again believer is justified. This is made especially plain in Romans 5:12-21, where we meet the phrase "justification of life" (5:18).

But the experience of people who lived in Palestine, where the great spiritual drama of salvation had its manifestation in history, was a unique experience. It can never be repeated. Thus too, as Acts discloses, those who lived in that land during these momentous

Harmony with God

times had some very special directions to follow along the pathway to membership in the Body of Christ, the Church.

This special status as members of Christ's spiritual body, which was unknown even to the most godly saint in Old Testament times, could only be reached in the way specified by Acts 2:38. Those who have made Acts 2:38 a normative experience, applicable to all believers during the present age of the Church, have not studied their Bibles with sufficient care. Acts 2:38; 8:12-17; 19:1-7; and 22:16 belong to a transitional period in Christian history and, as all these texts show, they are aimed at Palestinians *and no one else!*

Thus when Paul preaches to a Jewish audience *outside of Palestine* (in what was called the Diaspora [Dispersion]), he preaches the same message that he preached everywhere on the Gentile mission fields. As a result, in the synagogue at Antioch of Pisidia, we find him telling his Jewish hearers: "Therefore let it be known to you, brethren, that through this Man is preached to you the forgiveness of sins; and by Him everyone who believes *is justified* from all things from which you could not be justified by the law of Moses" (Acts 13:38-39).

Harmony with God and a full clearance before the bar of His justice—that is, fellowship with Him and security from eternal judgment—these are the benefits

Repentance in Palestine

that God offers to Jew and Gentile alike throughout the age of the Church, on the basis of faith alone.

But thanks to Acts and to the contrast it presents with the experience of Palestinian believers, we can appreciate the ease of our own acceptance with God at both the judicial and personal levels. On both these levels, when we are saved, we are accepted by faith alone.

—12—

REPENTANCE AND SOUND DOCTRINE

In concluding our study of repentance, it is appropriate that we come back to the Gospel of John. Our study began with the observation that John's silence about repentance makes it impossible to believe that he thought of it as a condition for eternal life.

Our review of the relevant Scriptures fully supports this deduction. Repentance is never presented in the NT as a condition for eternal life. Yet at the same time, repentance is an important theme in the Bible and, as part of God's revelation to man, we are called upon to preach it.

But our consideration of these passages, and of related themes like forgiveness of sins, gives us a new appreciation for the technique used by the Fourth Gospel. Let us think about this just a little bit again before we conclude this book.

The Simple Gospel

Harmony with God

What emerges from our study is the realization that the Gospel of John is a presentation of *the simple gospel* of Jesus Christ. John deliberately avoids the many possible complications that can sometimes cloud the simplicity of God's offer of life. He is wisely content to focus on the core issue, which is: *How can a person know that he possesses eternal life and that he will never perish under God's judgment?*

> "...THE GOSPEL OF JOHN, IS A PRESENTATION OF *THE SIMPLE GOSPEL* OF JESUS CHRIST. JOHN DELIBERATELY AVOIDS THE MANY POSSIBLE COMPLICATIONS THAT CAN SOMETIMES CLOUD THE SIMPLICITY OF GOD'S OFFER OF LIFE."

As we have seen, the failure to possess eternal life is the basis upon which men and women will be condemned to eternal hell (Rev 20:15). This means that eternal life is the critical consideration. How then can one possess it? The answer is the simple one given in the words of Jesus, who said, "Most assuredly, I say to you, he who believes in Me has everlasting life" (Jn 6:47). This is a theme John articulates over and over again, using mainly the words of our Lord Himself to do so.

Repentance and Sound Doctrine

Precisely because of his focus on the core issue of the gospel, John has nothing to say either about repentance or about the subject of an individual's experience of forgiveness. It should be evident that, even in John's day, which was by no means free from false doctrine (see 1 Jn 2:18-23; 4:1-6), this apostle felt it prudent to leave these auxiliary subjects alone in order to make his message unmistakably clear.

And it is when we turn to the book of Acts that we learn how freighted with complications both of these subjects are.

Doctrinal Complexity

The New Testament presentation of the doctrines of repentance and forgiveness possesses a complexity that the Church as a whole seems to have been unable to firmly grasp and retain. Let us recapitulate a moment.

Repentance and baptism, as we have seen, were conditions for forgiveness during the ministries of John the Baptist, of the apostles and of our Lord Jesus Himself. But this was only true for the Israelites of Palestine, who were called to national repentance by the Baptist and, after the crucifixion of Christ, were called again to repentance by the apostles (Acts 2:38; 3:19). Following baptism and forgiveness, the believing

Harmony with God

Israelite from Palestine could receive the gift of the Holy Spirit.

The Samaritan situation was similar, but probably not identical. We are nowhere told that forgiveness for the believing Samaritans waited on baptism, and very likely it did not. But the gift of the Spirit was received only after baptism just as with Palestinian Jews. God chose to bring the Samaritans into the Church in the same way as the Jews of Palestine, that is, by means of the gift of the Spirit following water baptism.

The Gentiles on the other hand, as well as (we infer) non-Palestinian Jews such as those in Antioch of Pisidia, received eternal life, forgiveness of sins and the gift of the Spirit at the moment of faith in Christ. Water baptism followed the bestowal of these blessings and did not precede any of them.

Obviously, the apostle John doesn't want to go into any of these issues. To do so would have either greatly lengthened his book or made it very confusing. The wisdom of the Spirit who inspired John is evident in his choice of subject matter.

In his one reference to forgiveness of sins (Jn 20:23), John is content to point to the authority of the apostles to regulate this experience. Acts 2:38 is a classic case of such regulation. The apostolic pronouncement in that verse proclaimed forgiveness of sins to be available to the repentant Israelite who was baptized. Any who

Repentance and Sound Doctrine

refused this apostolic prescription were *not forgiven*, that is, their sins were "retained" (Jn 20:23). They were thus excluded from fellowship with God until such time as they submitted to the apostolic conditions.

John and Justification

We might wonder, however, why John chose not to refer to justification by faith, which is obtained by faith alone just as is eternal life.

Two reasons for this may be suggested. First, a discussion of justification was unnecessary if the condition for receiving eternal life is made clear. The person who believes in Christ for eternal life also automatically receives justification by faith. A discussion of justification was not really needed.

But second, even more to the point is the observation that, as a piece of literature, John was writing a *Gospel.* Thus his literary intention is to allow the Lord Jesus Christ, whose career is the basis of this book, to speak the message in His own words. Therein lay the authority on which John is relying as he presents the basic Christian message. It was Jesus Himself, John is telling us, who offered eternal life on the basis of faith alone in Himself alone!

The evidence of the four Gospels certainly suggests to us that the Lord Jesus did not speak very often on

Harmony with God

the subject of justification. There are indeed a few passages where this subject seems implicit (one might cite Mt 5:20; Lk 14:14 and 20:35; Jn 5:28-29), but the allusion to this truth in these places usually goes unobserved. Nevertheless, there is one text where Jesus does speak explicitly of justification, and that text is a beautiful pre-Pauline presentation of grace versus works.

The passage, of course, is the one describing the Pharisee and the publican who went up to the temple to pray (Lk 18:9-14). According to our Lord, it was not the Pharisee, who paraded his good works before God, but the publican who "went down to his house *justified*" (18:14; italics added). It is striking that the publican's words, "God, be merciful to me a sinner" (Lk 18:13), employ a Greek word (*hilaskomai* = "to propitiate") from which are derived the Greek words for "propitiation" (*hilasmos*) and "mercy seat" (*hilasterion*). The publican's words thus can be understood as anticipating God's saving provision through the Messiah and could be translated, "God, be *propitiated* toward me a sinner."

A better pre-Pauline statement of the truth of justification through the propitiatory work of Christ, rather than by works, would be hard to imagine.

But although Jesus articulated the doctrine of justification in seed form, He chose to reveal this truth

Repentance and Sound Doctrine

most fully to the apostles, and above all to Paul, after His own ascension to God's right hand. By and large, justification by faith is one of those rich themes of which Jesus spoke when He said, "I still have many things to say to you, but you cannot bear them now. However, when He, the Spirit of truth, has come, He will guide you into all truth" (Jn 16:12-13a).

If, therefore, John was concentrating on the words of Jesus to communicate the gospel of salvation by faith, then his omission of a reference to justification is not only understandable but prudent. Part of his skill in penning this indispensable Gospel is his ability to "stay on message." As a result it is impossible to read his book without hearing again and again its simple, yet amazing offer of eternal life by faith in Christ. John allows this message to stand out without complication.

John 5:28-29

Since the Lord Jesus had evidently said little about justification, John could not make His words on this great theme the basis of his Gospel. So he chose not to refer to it directly at all. In one place in his Gospel, however, it is possible to see an implicit reference to justification.

In describing the two resurrections in 5:28-29, John speaks of those who come forth in "the resurrection

Harmony with God

of life" as "those who have done good," and those who come forth in "the resurrection of condemnation" (Greek = "judgment") as "those who have done evil." There is no qualification here at all (such as, "more good than evil" or vice versa), and we have no right to read it into the text.

Those who participate in the resurrection of life are presented as doers of good and *only* good. This implies that they possess a perfect righteousness before God, which of course is attainable only by means of justification (Rom 3:21-22).

By contrast, those who come forth in the resurrection of judgment (that is, at the Great White Throne) have done evil and *only* evil. They fit the Pauline claim, "There is none who does good, no, not one" (Rom 3:12).

Nevertheless, in John 5:28-29, the doctrine of justification by faith is only *implicit*. John does not expound it here or elsewhere in his writings.

Under the guidance of the Holy Spirit, therefore, John and the other original apostles allow Paul (the converted Pharisee!) to be God's chief spokesman for the wonderful truth that, when we believe in Christ, we are completely cleared of every charge of evil and possess the very righteousness of God by faith. As Paul says so simply, "But to him who *does not work* but *believes* on Him who justifies the ungodly, his faith is accounted for righteousness" (Rom 4:5; italics added).

Repentance and Sound Doctrine

Repentance to Life

Finally, it is worth considering the observation made by the believers at Jerusalem after they heard Peter's account of his visit with Cornelius. Their comment was: "Then God has also granted to the Gentiles repentance to life" (Acts 11:18).

Needless to say this text has been read as if it meant "repentance to *eternal* life"! It has then been urged that this shows that repentance is necessary for eternal salvation. But this view will not bear scrutiny.

To begin with, the word "eternal" is not really here. Although eternal life *can be* referred to by the word "life" alone (very notably in John 20:31 and elsewhere in the Fourth Gospel), we cannot make this assumption automatically. The word is a perfectly good Greek word for "life" in the various senses in which the language could use it. We must always interpret in context.

Secondly, if we thought that the reference in Acts 11:18 *was* a reference to *eternal* life, then we are left with a surprising and implausible idea in this context. We must infer in that case that the Jerusalem Christians just now realized that Gentiles could be eternally *saved!* But this is so unlikely as to be almost fantastic.

After all, had not the Lord Himself commanded the Gentile mission in His Great Commission to the apostles (Mt 28:19; Mk 16:15)? In fact, even the OT

Harmony with God

taught that Gentiles could be saved (see the quotations in Rom 15:8-11). In the Jerusalem church, of all places, this truth must surely have been known. Indeed, before he spoke, Peter is not criticized for *preaching* to Gentiles, but for *eating* with them (Acts 11:3)!

Peter had treated these Gentiles as though he found them fully acceptable since, apparently after his sermon, he had sat down to eat with them. But this implied that they were also fully acceptable to God, and yet all they had done was to repent of their paganism and believe in Christ. They had *not* become Jewish proselytes!

But the fact that they were indeed fully accepted by God had been signaled by His giving them, says Peter, "the same gift as He gave us when we believed on the Lord Jesus Christ" (Acts 11:17). In this respect, they were more readily blessed than the Palestinian Jews had been!

We must remember that the Jews at Pentecost did not get the gift of the Spirit until after baptism. But God did not require even this of Cornelius in order for him to be baptized by God's Spirit. It was thus evident that the Gentiles had entered the same "life experience" that believing Jews enjoyed, that is, they were fully blessed by the God with whom they were now obviously in harmony. *We* might say, "They entered into the Christian life."

Repentance and Sound Doctrine

Here we need to recall the words of the father of the Prodigal Son. Upon his son's return home, the experiential separation of father and son had ended, so that his dad can say to his unhappy older boy, "Your brother was *dead and is alive again*, and was lost and is found" (Lk 15:32: italics added).

Repentance, we may say, is the wayward sinner's first step toward "coming to life" after his experience of alienation and separation from God. Experientially this is true both for the unsaved sinner and for the saved sinner. Coming home to God, and enjoying His presence, is a form of resurrection and it is a true and vivid experience of *life!* As Paul would put it later, "For if you live according to the flesh you will *die*, but if by the Spirit you put to death the deeds of the body, you will *live*" (Rom 8:13; italics added).

The believers at Jerusalem knew what the father of the Prodigal Son was referring to. But they were surprised that "life" in this sense could be enjoyed totally apart from any conditions related to the Mosaic law. The truth they acknowledged here, however, was later to come under challenge (see the view of the believing Pharisees in Acts 15:5), and it was to be officially resolved by the Jerusalem Council (Acts 15:4-29). But at this moment, the believers are delighted and "they glorified God" (Acts 11:18) because the Gentiles had entered into full and genuine Christian living.

Harmony with God

Christian Applications

A number of repentance passages that relate to Christian experience have not yet been mentioned. Let us look quickly at these.

In 2 Corinthians 7:8-12 Paul is pleased to note that his previous letter to the church had produced "repentance" (2 Cor 7:9, 10), leading to a correction of the situation for which he had rebuked them. This correction was thus a "salvation" (Greek = "deliverance") from the former situation and from its undesirable consequences.

But not all the problems at Corinth had been straightened out by Paul's letter. Yet he hopes that he will not have to come to them in a spirit of rebuke and discipline to deal with those who are involved in sins of which they have not yet repented (2 Cor 12:20-21). Naturally he is appealing for immediate repentance in such cases.

In 2 Timothy 2:24-26 Paul encourages Timothy to have a humble attitude when confronting misguided Christians whom the devil has ensnared in false doctrine. He must not regard any confrontation as a "quarrel" (Greek = "he must not fight"), but as an opportunity to help them to reach a God-given repentance for their false doctrine.

In the famous text in Hebrews 6:1-6, Paul is thinking

Repentance and Sound Doctrine

of Christians who have turned away from their Christian faith and returned to some form of Judaism. He believes such people lay a basis for repenting all over again from the "dead works" of the law (Heb 6:1), which they had abandoned when they trusted in Christ alone. He understands that those who do such a thing are very "hard" spiritually and that no human effort will succeed in renewing them "to repentance" (Heb 6:6), that is, restoring them to the point where they were when they abandoned "dead works" for God's grace. But the impossibility he refers to (Heb 6:4) does not apply to God, of course, and he *hints* that God's discipline may bring about their return just like the burning of a field opens the way for it to be reused for cultivation (Heb 6:7-8).

Finally, in Hebrews 12:17, Esau is said to have "found no place for repentance." "Place" here probably means something like "suitable occasion." (cf. the very similar meaning of "place" in Hebrews 8:7, i.e., "no *occasion* would have been sought.") The point here is that Esau's repentance was untimely—it was too late, because the blessing he sought with tears was irrevocably lost. (The Greek makes clear that "it" in this verse refers to the "blessing," not to the "repentance.") Implied is the truth that at the Judgment Seat of Christ, if we have become aware of lost heirship or rewards, no amount of sorrow for our failures

Harmony with God

will avail to regain these things.

None of these texts, however, are dealing with the way a person obtains eternal salvation. Instead they illustrate some of the many forms that *Christian repentance* may have to take.

Conclusion

Repentance definitely can and should bring glory to God, as it did at Jerusalem in Acts 11:18. And it does so when it is properly understood, not as a condition for eternal salvation, but as the means by which we can reach harmony with our Maker no matter how far we have strayed from him.

The unsaved man can find in repentance a road that leads him to faith in Christ and to fellowship with the Father in heaven. Even when he comes to faith in Christ *before repentance*, as he later repents of long continued sins he can find fellowship and harmony with his Savior and with his God.

And a Christian who has walked with God for years, and then has left that path to go off into sin (like the Prodigal Son), can always repent and come home to his heavenly Father.

Someday, too, the nation of Israel will repent and will recover their special relationship to the God of Abraham, Isaac and Jacob. The prophet Zechariah vividly describes Israel's repentance as a time of

Repentance and Sound Doctrine

national mourning (Zech 12:10-14). That is still to come.

Most definitely, we have every reason to thank God for allowing sinners like ourselves to repent and to find harmony and joy in His presence, after days or months or years of waywardness and rebellion. Like everything else God does for us, this is possible only because He gave His Son to be the propitiation for our sins. It is one of the numberless benefits of the cross of Christ.

But as wonderful as it is, there remains one thing repentance cannot do for us. It cannot give us eternal life or security from eternal judgment. If eternal life depended on our repentance, we could never know whether our status before God was secure, since at anytime (if we know our own hearts!) we could wander away and need to repent again.

Those who teach that repentance is necessary for eternal salvation can have no true assurance of their eternal destiny. And if they claim to have this, they are either fooling themselves or us or both!

Thank God there is only one answer to the question, "What must I do to be saved?" That, of course, is the answer not only of Paul and all the apostles, but of Jesus Himself. The answer is: "Believe!"

Repentance is not a part of that answer. It never has been and never will be. But we should keep firmly in mind the lovely truth that repentance is always the first step when we need to come home again!

Scripture Index

ISAIAH
Isa 9:19 94

JEREMIAH
Jer 21:12-14 94
Jer 22:6-7 94
Jer 48:45 94

EZEKIEL
Ezek 15:1-8 94
Ezek 18:21, 23 61
Ezek 18:30b-32 61

DANIEL
Daniel, Book of 59

HOSEA
Hosea 8:14 94

AMOS
Amos 1:4, 7, 10, 12, 14 94
Amos 2:2, 5 94

JONAH
Jonah, Book of 79, 80
Jonah 3:10 .... 50, 78
Jonah 3:4 .... 50, 78
Jonah 3:5 50
Jonah 3:7ff 50

NAHUM
Nahum, Book of 63, 79
Nahum 1:6 94

ZEPHANIAH
Zeph 1:18 94

ZECHARIAH
Zech 12:10-14 123

MATTHEW

Matthew, Book of	14
Mt 3:2	89
Mt 3:5	96
Mt 3:8	89, 92
Mt 3:10	93
Mt 3:11	89
Mt 4:17	89
Mt 5:20	114
Mt 9:13	89
Mt 11:20-24	80
Mt 12:41	79
Mt 24	59
Mt 24:38-39	58
Mt 27:25	96
Mt 28:19	117

MARK

Mark, Book of	14
Mk 1:4	89, 94
Mk 1:5	95
Mk 1:8	90
Mk 1:15	89
Mk 2:17	89
Mk 6:12	89
Mk 16:15	117

LUKE

Luke, Book of	14
Lk 3:3	89, 94, 96
Lk 3:8	89, 92, 93
Lk 3:9	93
Lk 3:10	92
Lk 3:10-14	92
Lk 3:12	92
Lk 3:14	92
Lk 5:32	89
Lk 10:13-14	80
Lk 11:32	79
Lk 13:1	51
Lk 13:1-5	49, 51, 60
Lk 13:2-3	51

Lk 13:3	52
Lk 13:4-5	52
Lk 13:5	52
Lk 14:14	114
Lk 15	19, 23, 24, 26, 29, 31, 39
Lk 15:1-3	24
Lk 15:1-10	23, 31
Lk 15:2	24
Lk 15:4	24
Lk 15:5	25
Lk 15:4-7	39
Lk 15:6	24, 25
Lk 15:7	25
Lk 15:8	27
Lk 15:8-10	39
Lk 15:9-10	28
Lk 15:10	28
Lk 15:11-24	31, 39
Lk 15:12	44
Lk 15:13	34
Lk 15:14-16	49
Lk 15:17-19	32
Lk 15:17-21	49
Lk 15:20	33
Lk 15:21	33
Lk 15:23	33
Lk 15:23-24	33
Lk 15:25-32	26, 39
Lk 15:27	39
Lk 15:28	40
Lk 15:29	43
Lk 15:29a	41
Lk 15:29b	42
Lk 15:30	46
Lk 15:31	44
Lk 15:32	45, 119
Lk 17:3-4	72
Lk 17:10	43
Lk 18:9-14	114
Lk 18:13	114
Lk 18:14	114

LUKE (cont'd)
Lk 20:35 114
Lk 24:47 .... 8, 65, 78
Lk 24:6-7 28

JOHN
John, Book of 14, 66
Jn 1:29 68
Jn 1:35-40 90
Jn 3:3 .... 69, 102
Jn 3:16 .... 68, 98, 99
Jn 4 54
Jn 5:24 .... 98, 99
Jn 5:28-29 .... 114, 115, 116
Jn 6:47 .... 98, 99, 110
Jn 7:39 .... 90, 102
Jn 9 54
Jn 14:17 102
Jn 16:12-13a 115
Jn 20:23 .... 66, 112, 113
Jn 20:30-31 .... 2, 3, 13, 67, 99
Jn 20:31 .... 68, 117

ACTS
Acts, Book of 80, 96, 97, 102, 105, 107, 111
Acts 2 .... 102, 104
Acts 2:36 98
Acts 2:36-38 101
Acts 2:37 .... 98, 102
Acts 2:38 .... 8, 65, 98, 99, 102, 106, 111, 112
Acts 3:19 .... 8, 65, 111
Acts 5:31 .... 65, 89
Acts 8 98
Acts 8:12-17 106
Acts 8:14-17 104
Acts 8:22 65
Acts 9 100
Acts 9:5 100
Acts 9:17 100
Acts 10 .... 83, 84
Acts 10:2 80
Acts 10:34-43 82

Acts 10:36, 43 95
Acts 10:42-43 81
Acts 10:43 .... 65, 95
Acts 10:43-44 83
Acts 10:44 81
Acts 11:3 118
Acts 11:4-17 82
Acts 11:14 81
Acts 11:17 118
Acts 11:18 .... 10, 65, 117, 119, 122
Acts 13:24 .... 65, 89
Acts 13:38 65
Acts 13:38-39 106
Acts 13:48 82
Acts 15:4-29 119
Acts 15:5 119
Acts 16:27-31 55
Acts 16:30 1
Acts 16:31 .... 2, 3, 29, 55
Acts 17:22-31 .... 84, 85
Acts 17:30 .... 8, 65
Acts 17:30-31 84
Acts 17:34 85
Acts 19 .... 97, 98
Acts 19:1-7 106
Acts 19:2 .... 90, 91, 97, 103, 104
Acts 19:3 .... 91, 97
Acts 19:4 .... 53, 65, 89, 90, 91, 104
Acts 19:5 .... 91, 98
Acts 19:6 .... 91, 98
Acts 20:21 .... 65, 86
Acts 21:9 17
Acts 22 .... 100, 101
Acts 22:3 100
Acts 22:8 101
Acts 22:16 .... 100, 106
Acts 26 100
Acts 26:18 65
Acts 26:20 .... 65, 86

ROMANS
Rom 1:21 20

ROMANS (cont'd)

Rom 2:4-5 62
Rom 3:12 116
Rom 3:20 69
Rom 3:21-22 116
Rom 3:21-26 105
Rom 4:5 116
Rom 5:1 105
Rom 5:12-21 105
Rom 5:18 105
Rom 8:13 119
Rom 8:31-34 105
Rom 15:8-11 118

1 CORINTHIANS

1 Cor 11:5 17
1 Cor 11:10 28
1 Cor 11:30 16
1 Cor 12:13 102
1 Cor 13 23

2 CORINTHIANS

2 Cor 5:19 71
2 Cor 7:8-12 120
2 Cor 7:9-10 120
2 Cor 12:20-21 120

EPHESIANS

Eph 2:1 95
Eph 2:8-9 69
Eph 3:10 28

1 THESSALONIANS

1 Thess 1:9 85
1 Thess 5 59
1 Thess 5:2-3 58

1 TIMOTHY

1 Tim 1:20 17

2 TIMOTHY

2 Tim 2:24-26 120

TITUS
Titus 3:5 69

HEBREWS
Hebrews, Book of 14
Heb 1:14 28
Heb 6:1 121
Heb 6:1-6 120
Heb 6:4 121
Heb 6:6 121
Heb 6:7-8 121
Heb 8:7 121
Heb 11 23
Heb 12:3-11 15
Heb 12:17 121
Heb 12:22-23 28

JAMES
James 2 15

2 PETER
2 Peter, Book of 14
2 Peter 1:19 27
2 Peter 3 .... 57, 59, 60, 61
2 Peter 3:3-4 58
2 Peter 3:6 58
2 Peter 3:9 .... 57, 61
2 Peter 3:10 58
2 Peter 3:15 62

1 JOHN
1 John, Book of 18
1 Jn 1:9 18
1 Jn 2:12-14 18
1 Jn 2:18-23 111
1 Jn 2:2 .... 68, 71
1 Jn 2:21 18
1 Jn 2:24 18
1 Jn 2:28 18
1 Jn 3:1 32
1 Jn 4:1-6 111
1 Jn 4:21 46

1 JOHN (cont'd)
1 Jn 5:1 .... 47, 99, 100

2 JOHN
2 John, Book of 18
2 Jn 8 15

3 JOHN
3 John, Book of 18

JUDE
Jude, Book of 14

REVELATION
Revelation, Book of 14, 20, 21
Rev 2 18
Rev 2:4 16
Rev 2:5 16
Rev 2:8-11 18
Rev 2:12-17 16
Rev 2:14-15 16
Rev 2:16 16
Rev 2:20 .... 16, 17
Rev 2:21 16
Rev 2:22 .... 16, 17
Rev 3 18
Rev 3:1 15
Rev 3:2 15
Rev 3:3 15
Rev 3:7-13 18
Rev 3:14-22 14
Rev 3:19 15
Rev 8 19
Rev 9 19
Rev 9:13-19 19
Rev 9:18 19
Rev 9:20-21 19
Rev 11:3-13 59
Rev 16:9 19
Rev 16:11 .... 19, 20
Rev 20:11-14 67
Rev 20:12 67

REVELATION (cont'd)
Rev 20:15 .... 67, 110